COMING OUT

EMERGING FROM SHAME AND CONFUSION,
OPENING THE DOOR TO LIGHT AND LOVE

A TRUE STORY OF FAITH, HOPE,
AND PERSEVERANCE

DAVID L. LOWRY

Trilogy Christian Publishers
A Wholly Owned Subsidary of Trinity Broadcasting Network
2442 Michelle Drive
Tustin, CA 92780

For information, address Trilogy Christian Publishing
Rights Department, 2442 Michelle Drive, Tustin, Ca 92780.
Trilogy Christian Publishing/ TBN and colophon are trademarks of Trinity Broadcasting Network.

For information about special discounts for bulk purchases, please contact Trilogy Christian Publishing.

Manufactured in the United States of America

Trilogy Disclaimer: The views and content expressed in this book are those of the author and may not necessarily reflect the views and doctrine of Trilogy Christian Publishing or the Trinity Broadcasting Network.

10 9 8 7 6 5 4 3 2 1

Library of Congress Cataloging-in-Publication Data is available.

ISBN 978-1-64088-459-5 (Print Book)
ISBN 978-1-64088-460-1 (ebook)

WHAT PEOPLE ARE SAYING ABOUT *COMING OUT*

Lots of people aren't going to like this book. Some won't think it's confrontational enough. Others won't think it's accepting enough. But if you like authentic stories of people struggling to live out their beliefs with integrity, then you just might love this book!

—Philip S. Tuttle, president and CEO of Walk Thru the Bible

David's story is a heart-wrenching—yet astonishingly hopeful—story of redemption. He found his identity in the God he loves through all the pain and soul searching. And I believe you will too, if you let his journey impact yours.

—Dave Rodriguez, senior pastor, Grace Church, Indianapolis

I highly recommend this book to anyone who is looking for inspiration to overcome an identity crisis, faith crisis, or relational crisis. I was so moved by the honest heartfelt story of David's life. He shared with tenderness the depth of friendship that nurtured him through finding his faith and healing in Jesus. Everyone will find themselves in this book in one of the many significant characters that God used to bring redemption to a broken life.

—Linda Znachko, author, *He Knows Your Name: How One Abandoned Baby Inspired Me To Say Yes To God*

Some truths are best carried through the simplicity of someone just telling their story. With refreshing courage and authenticity, David gently welcomes each of us to open a door to the possibility of a God who refuses to be limited by our political affiliation, religious doctrine, or sexual history. As you read, you just might encounter a redemptive God who can rewrite your life story in better ways than you thought possible.

—Erik Fish, author and creative leadership catalyst

Coming Out gripped my attention as I experienced David Lowry's cyclic journey—from confusion and despair to hope and temporary bliss, then facing disappointment and winding up back at confusion, but thankfully ending with lasting hope. We all traverse this repetitive circle of emotions and search for the elusive "it." David eventually found "it" and gives us all hope as we share his unusual-but-relatable journey. His story doesn't have a fairy-tale ending, but does have what we all long for: unconditional love!

—Paul Gray, author, *Convertible Conversations*

Rare is the opportunity to truly capture the inside thoughts, feelings, and motivations of a person who has emerged, by God's grace, from a destructive and pain-filled lifestyle. David's story is a window that transports the reader to delve into an inimitable life narrative rich with detail, deep with emotion, and saturated with hope. Laughter, tears, introspection—all will be part of the journey that unfolds with each page. This honest glimpse of one man's struggles closely connects the reader to a genuine and sincere person whose reality involved great suffering, a falling away, a desperate search, and a glorious restoration.

—Lori Erickson Trump, pastor, Living Truth Church

I have been in ministry for over forty years and have read many life-changing books, but this book is of a different significance. This is a life-changing book that brings hope and freedom to those who read it and have a desire to be free from their past or present situation. God answers our prayers through people. David has a powerful testimony that I believe has been ordained for such a time as this. His story brings to light the grace of God through his deliverance.

—Dr. Johnnie Blount, CEO, Bridging the Gap Ministries

When it comes to defining a "good autobiography," I point you to David Lowry's, *Coming Out*. By writing about his relationships, his beliefs, and his "Hindsight Revelations," David Lowry allows readers to understand his definition of *Coming Out,* which is about discovering personal identity and a sense of belonging. If you are someone who has trouble fitting in or feels out of place, I highly recommend this book.

—Ben

Coming Out is a great book that tells one man's testimony of a really hard life with lots of deep lows, but some high mountaintop experiences too. It will challenge you personally on many levels. My heart hurt for David as I read through the struggles he faced, but I rejoiced each time he overcame a battle. By being willing to let the world see the raw reality of his life, David gives us a glimpse of hope—seeing how God can and will use our trials and low spots is extremely encouraging. I look forward to re-reading *Coming Out* and passing it on.

—Rachel

Once I picked up David's book, I could not stop reading it. I felt like I was sitting across the table from him as he told his story. And although my own story may be very different in some ways, my heart resonated with his desire for love, acceptance, significance, and security, because at the end of the day I believe that is what every human heart longs for.

—Lisa

DEDICATION

To my father and mother,
  who obediently and faithfully took me to church every Sunday to have the seeds of God's Word implanted in my heart.

To my Ms. Ruth,
  who came along years later to water those dormant seeds and nurture my spiritual growth.

To all of my bird feeders (you know who you are), who nursed me back to health and never gave up on me.

And most importantly—to my best friend, Jesus, whose love has never failed me and never will.

* * *

I'd also like to dedicate this book to my three children who have brought great joy and many blessings to my life.
  May your destiny be fulfilled to God's glory and may the Father's loving presence be with you always.

Love, Dad

CONTENTS

PART TWO: LEARNING TO FLY

ACKNOWLEDGMENTS

Thanks to Anj Marie Riffel of Kingdom Heart Publishing, for her writing partnership, as well as editing, design, and publishing assistance. And to her excellent team of proofreaders, Lydia Benda and Michelle C. Booth.

Thanks to Erik Fish, for offering wise counsel and valuable insights throughout the writing process.

Thanks to my management team, Angela and Tina, not only for their assistance with this project, but also for seeing me through many highs and lows.

Thanks to everyone who has been instrumental in encouraging me and helping me share this story.

And thanks to my prayer warriors, who have faithfully lifted up this endeavor before the Lord.

NOTE TO READERS

Am I gay? Am I not gay? I have lived my life both ways—and learned that the truth is something different altogether. I'm grateful to have found freedom, a gift I hope to share through telling my story. *Coming Out* is a journey of discovery through faith, hope, and perseverance. It's about relationships and forgiveness, sexuality and identity, secrets and revelations. And it's a love story too, though maybe not the kind you'd expect.

Never in my wildest dreams would I have thought of writing a book about my life. People seemed to keep suggesting this to me, but I had mixed emotions. My life has been messy in a lot of ways. But it's also a beautiful story of redemption and transformation. That's the part I'm excited to share. I hope to shine a light for anyone who feels alone in the dark.

If you're in pain, wrestling with confusion, or hoping to help someone who's struggling—this book is for you. Fair warning: it may poke at your comfort zone. We'll be covering some controversial ground. You may not always agree with my perspectives, but I hope you'll read with an open mind and soft heart.

Everyone's journey is different, with its own share of difficulty. After enduring abuse and rejection from a young age, I spent much of my life feeling like God was displeased with me and never around when I needed him most. (It was actually quite the opposite, but we'll get to that.) Thankfully, somewhere in the suffering, I began to recognize the lies that had distorted my world for far too long.

Coming Out is about much more than the title may imply. It's the story of a boy who felt like a disappointment, who grew up to be a man tormented by pain. Through it all, I remained determined to discover the truth. *Coming Out* is about emerging from the dark closet of shame and confusion—and opening the door to light and love.

I invite you to begin a quest of your own as you turn the page. I should note that I've changed some of the names and details to protect people's privacy, but the core is the truth as I know it. After each chapter, I've included some "hindsight revelations." These are brief reflections on how I see things now, with the perspective time brings. I pray that my testimony will serve as a springboard for you to dive deeper into your own search for truth.

With love,

David

PART ONE

FALLING

Like a bird that wanders from her nest,
so is a man who wanders from his home.
—Proverbs 27:8

Keep me as the apple of your eye; hide
me in the shadow of your wings.
—Psalm 17:8

IF you see a helpless baby bird that has fallen from its nest, should you help it or let it be?

A young bird might fall for many reasons—some species may be pushed by an aggressive nest-mate. This injured hatchling is especially vulnerable to predators.

It's a myth that the mother will reject her baby if you try to help, but the wrong type of intervention can do more harm than good. The best way to help is to reunite the baby with its mother. Who better knows how to protect and care for her child?

Chances are good that the mother is nearby, even if she cannot be immediately seen.

I was once much like this baby bird. I fell. I was lost.

I couldn't find God.

1

THE FALL

AGE 12

IT WAS THE SUMMER I would never forget—*could* never forget. It was the summer that my future teetered precariously at the top of a ledge.

School was out, the garden planted. Our farm was bursting forth with life—rows and rows of crops as far as the eye could see. It was one of those days so thick with heat that you could barely take in a full breath. Everyone was in the fields cutting and raking hay.

I was still a kid by today's measure, but I'd hit double digits, so I was expected to do increasingly more work on the farm. Long days in the sun had lightened my blond hair to near white and darkened my usually fair skin. (Funny how exposure to the same catalyst can result in opposite reactions: one gets lighter while the other gets darker. I suppose this can happen to the soul as well.)

There must have been a lot of work this particular day because Grandfather was helping out. He seldom did any work on the farm since a stroke early in life had left him partially paralyzed on one side—and disgruntled all over. I felt pride well up in me when Grandfather chose me to unload the hay from the wagon. This was the only chore on the farm that I did better than my brothers and I was desperate to prove myself worthy to hang with the men.

In those years, we shot hay out of a baler and laid them like bricks on a wagon. I watched with a sigh as the green Oliver tractor arrived (only Olivers were allowed on our farm since Grandfather deemed it a sin to use anything else). The wagon was piled high, ready for me to unload. I wasn't allowed to back the hay in. Grandfather said I never did it right.

The massive doors of our weatherworn barn were opened wide, like a giant mouth eager for lunch. Conversely, I wasn't the least bit eager, but tried to ready myself with a deep breath. How I loved the smell of alfalfa! Sweeter than fresh-cut grass. I hated everything else about hay season. It was hot, itchy, sweaty—seemed never-ending. I wished I could play and ride my bike instead. Or watch soaps with Grandmother in the cool haven of the redbrick house. Of course, that was frowned upon by the men of the family as a "girl thing." I was expected to take my place among my gender.

I grabbed a quick drink, opening my mouth under the spigot of our Coleman jug. The nice, cold water tried valiantly to offer respite in the war against heat. Meanwhile, Grandfather stood a few feet away wearing his typical attire: striped overalls, button-down shirt, straw hat, and dusty old boots. A wooden cane was an ever-present extension of his right hand, like Captain Hook with a stick. In spite of the stroke and his age, Grandfather was a commanding figure. About six-foot-two, he seemed huge to me—not overweight, but hefty. His chiseled features made him look like an ancient statue come to life.

Apart from our piercing blue eyes, Grandfather and I had nothing in common. He picked on me more than the other grandkids and always called me Corky. Not sure why, but I could tell he didn't mean it affectionately. Maybe he didn't like me because I was left-handed. People used to say that meant you were "of the devil." Plus, I had blond hair, not brown, like everyone else in the family. That seemed to bother him too. Whatever the reason, we never hit it off.

Grandfather yelled a lot, and today was no exception. He hollered at me to quit loafing, using his cane to direct me to my spot. A farmhand named Ray backed the hay into the barn as I wedged myself between the wagon and the hay elevator. It's unfortunate that Ray, of all people, was the only witness to what was about to happen. I've since wondered if this day marked me as easy prey in his mind. Ray would later become one of my abusers.

Just as I was getting into the rhythm of unloading bales, Grandfather told me to step back. I knew there was a hay chute behind me—a fifteen-foot drop to the lower level. I looked over my shoulder, eyeing the concrete below. Shouting over the noise of the equipment, I yelled, "I can't go back any farther. I'll fall!"

Grandfather ignored this, lowered his voice to a growl, and repeated emphatically, "Step. Back." Next, I saw his ugly brown cane come at me, forcing me backward.

I don't remember actually falling, just the moment right before. Then everything went black. I'm not sure if I lost consciousness and don't know how long I laid there.

When I opened my eyes, Grandfather was still there. He was leaning over the chute, heaving in peals of laughter. Our blue eyes met. His felt like icy daggers. They pierced the once tranquil waters of my soul, creating a ripple effect that would change my life forever. To this day, the contortions of his face are emblazoned in my memory. His mannerisms told me this was no accident. My grandfather may have been a pawn, but the devil was at play. With the wind knocked out of me, I struggled to sit up, gasping for air. I looked around in a daze and felt something wet seeping through the back of my shirt. At first, I thought I was bleeding, but then realized I'd landed in cow manure. You get used to that smell living on a dairy farm, but it nauseated me now.

I looked up again and saw that Grandfather was gone. I needed to get out of there.

Miraculously, I had no physical injuries. I slowly got up, walked out of the barn, and headed toward safety. When I got close to home, it was suddenly all too much. I lost it and started crying. Weeping turned to wailing, louder with every step. Mom came running out to meet me halfway and scooped me up in a hug. We were both trembling.

"What in the world happened, son?" she asked.

I could barely form an intelligible sentence, but between sobs I managed, "I fell...he pushed me." Mom didn't ask who. Maybe she didn't need to.

By that time, Ray had come over to see if I was all right. I don't remember what was said, if anything. Mom and I walked the rest of the way home in silence.

Safely inside, we waited for the bathtub to fill up. Mom added Epsom salts to the water. I stepped in and soaked for a long time, wondering what kind of a boy I must be for Grandfather to hate me so much. I decided it must be my fault.

Somehow, I deserved this, I thought.

To further solidify this belief, my father never checked on me. Never said one word about it. In fact, no one in our family ever spoke of the incident. I'm not sure if my brothers even knew anything had happened—I sure wasn't going to bring it up. I didn't tell a soul for nearly fifty years.

That afternoon, farm work continued as though nothing had happened, except I got the rest of the day off. And Grandfather? He assumed his usual place as King of the Farm, sitting under the locust tree in his rusty old chair, sipping iced tea as Grandmother waited on him hand and foot.

HINDSIGHT REVELATIONS:
IDENTITY FORMATION

When I think over the pivotal events of my life, this one looms large. How could a young boy process such a traumatic event? I still don't have any answers as to why my grandfather forced me backward, nor what his true intentions were. I wasn't physically harmed, but emotionally, I was broken and bruised.

My grandfather's explicit rejection, coupled with my father's passive response, caused me to question my worth. These men were figureheads for my identity, and both of them seemed to be telling me that I didn't measure up. A child relies on mentors to protect—not to harm, not to ignore.

And what about God? Where was he that day? I would find out many years later, but for most of my life, I thought he had abandoned me. I thought he'd sided with the others, concluding that I was a colossal disappointment.

So confusion set in. My identity had fallen with me down that chute and hadn't fared so well. If I wasn't good enough as is, who should I become? I'd tried to be like my role models and obviously failed. I can trace so many of my choices to the thought patterns that took root this day. I yearned to be loved and accepted. I desperately craved the approval of men.

2

LIFE ON THE FARM

MY FIRST TWELVE YEARS

GROWING UP mid-century on a dairy farm in southwestern Pennsylvania was an experience I didn't fully appreciate until later in life. It was hard work, but there was so much wonder, beauty, and life to behold. Family was at the core of nearly everything we did.

My mother was a sassy brunette with wind-chime laughter that never failed to soothe my soul. Educated as a nurse, she was a loving caretaker and stayed home with us until I went to high school. Mom was also the disciplinarian, and I got my fair share of swats from her wooden paddle. But I didn't hold it against her. She was the one I went to when I needed anything.

Father was a large man, probably even larger in my memories, as I was always looking up at him. He was six-two, with a husky build like his father. He worked the farm all his life, taking the labor over after Grandfather's midlife stroke. My father rose with the roosters each morning to tend to his cows. I knew he loved me, but often wondered if he loved those cows more. Father was typically quiet—physically present, but emotionally distant and seemingly aloof, especially in the eyes of a child who craved demonstrative affection.

Although my father wasn't at ease in showing love to me (probably how he was raised), he absolutely adored his bride.

My parents were lavishly in love with each other. Could have made a movie of their marriage—it was certainly one that I tried to model later in life.

My oldest brother was six years older than I was. He was the first grandchild, so you can imagine the fuss over him. He also ended up being the shortest, a fact I still like to rib him about today. My middle brother, three years my senior, was the pot stirrer among us boys. He would often start a tussle over something then move slyly to the side, leaving my older brother and me to fight it out.

Our family farm had been passed down from father to eldest son for more than five generations. Nestled in a valley dotted with several white barns, it was a classic scene. The crowning glory was a magnificent redbrick Civil War–era homestead with a stately front porch and white picket fence. My grandparents' castle.

If you walked out the front door of Grandfather's house, crossed a dirt road, and followed a path to the wooden foot-bridge over the creek, you'd come to our white two-bedroom, one-bath house. Mounted on a hill to keep watch over the pasture fields, it had been built as a farmhand house back in the day.

I loved to roam the farm for hours on end, looking for treasures and adventure like Davy Crockett or the Lone Ranger. When I was about ten, Dad bought me a pony and I would ride that thing from sunup to sundown. No matter how many times she threw me off, I got back on. Ponies are stubborn—guess I was too. Eventually, I graduated to a horse. I especially loved riding bareback, steering her by the mane as we galloped over streams. Never saw my dad get so mad as he did for running her without a saddle. I solved this by making sure he was out of sight when I rode her.

I could be very demonstrative. As a kid, you never want to hear your parents fight. Mine rarely did (far as I know), but one night I heard them arguing in the yard. It upset me so much that I climbed to the attic for a suitcase, loaded it with clothes, and walked out the back door. My parents looked bewildered as I marched determinedly across the yard. They asked where I was going. Obviously I had no idea, but firmly declared that I was leaving because they were fighting. Then we all went back inside and that was that. Not sure who learned what lesson, but I never saw my parents argue again.

On the whole, we seemed like a picture-perfect, all-American family in my younger years. But farm life started to shift as we got older—less fun, more work. Our farm was a man's world that ran on sweat and bravado. Chores were never-ending, all done after school and before supper, which was on the table promptly each evening at five thirty. Nearly everything we ate was raised or grown on the farm.

Looking around the table, I decided I must have drawn a wild card from my family's DNA deck. My brothers were strapping and tough, while I was slight and sensitive. Family meals were like an eating competition. Stacks of flapjacks. Slabs of steak. The more you ate, the more manly you proved to be. The faster you ate, the better chance you had of playing for a bit. Mother wouldn't let me get up until I ate every last lima bean, so I would often be the only one left at the table. I tried feeding my limas to the dog, but he didn't want them either. My brother finally taught me the trick of slathering them with mayonnaise to get them down.

After everyone finished supper, it was back to the barn for the final milking. I would try to sneak off to the big red house to see Grandma, who would covertly treat me to freshly baked pie or cookies. I remember feeling so special being the only one there, but found out later in life that she did this for my brothers and cousins too. She was a wonderful woman of God who loved all her grandchildren equally.

Sundays were my favorite day of the week. Except for church, that is. Seemed like a long, boring waste of time. We had to get dressed in our Sunday best so we'd look fit to attend the local Presbyterian Church. First, we'd go to Sunday school to memorize stuff like the Ten Commandments, then everyone filed into a church service at eleven o'clock. Our family always sat in the same pew. It was the same with most families—heaven help any newcomer who might unknowingly sit in your pew.

This was the church where my mom and dad met. Mom was two years older than Dad, so when they started courting, it had been quite the talk of the town. As the only girl in her family, Mom grew up as the darling of four very protective brothers. Can't imagine what Dad must have gone through to earn their approval. Mom was raised on a farm too. With its picturesque southern mansion, it looked like the set of *Gone with the Wind.* My cousins and I loved swinging from the branches of the enormous weeping willow tree in the front yard. Mom's mother hosted a family gathering here every other Sunday. She wasn't the feel-good kind of woman my other grandmother was, but still nice in her own way. Mom's father passed away before I was born, so I never got to meet him. This side of the family intrigued me. They were more educated and seemed excitingly cultured. Some of them even smoked, which struck me as incredibly fashionable. Only one brother was a farmer and the rest were thriving businessmen. I hoped to be more like them one day.

On opposite Sundays, we gathered with Dad's family at the big red house. My dad had identical twin sisters who married two brothers (strange but true!). There were sixteen grandchildren, all close in age—a houseful and then some.

Sunday dinners were the only time our family prayed out loud. Either Grandfather or Dad would lead us in the same prayer every time. After a full feast, we would head to the pasture for softball.

No matter which grandma's house, no matter which Sunday, the festivities always came to a halt for the four o'clock milkings. Such was life on a dairy farm, but I really can't complain. My early years were good, better than most I suspect.

But against the backdrop of this almost idyllic picture of childhood, life started getting confusing as I grew older. There was the incident with Grandfather. And a growing distance with my dad and brothers. I began to feel more and more different, no matter how hard I tried to fit in. As I approached my teenage years, this insecurity did not serve me well in the face of dangers I never saw coming.

HINDSIGHT REVELATIONS:
WHAT IS NORMAL?

While I may have felt different from my more demonstrably masculine brothers, and like a disappointment to my grandfather, I wouldn't say I felt *abnormal* as a child. That came later.

Of course, these were different times than we're living in now. I didn't even know gay was a thing. But I don't think I was out of line with my peers. There were plenty of typical "boy" activities that I enjoyed. Then again, I loved cooking, was highly imaginative, and didn't possess the physical prowess of my brothers—so maybe I wasn't normal. Does being different have to mean something more?

What is normal anyway? Are our likes and dislikes reliable indicators of sexual identity?

Culturally speaking, we tend to celebrate individuality and embrace a beautiful spectrum of dispositions, personalities, physical attributes, interests, and talents. Exploration outside of traditional gender roles still seems to perpetuate certain assumptions, but the general response has changed to one of encouragement and acceptance of anything goes. This is a positive change in some respects, but does today's culture present alternative sexuality as an option or predisposition before it even hits most kids' radars?

I can only speak from my own story and testify that I am much more than the sum of my interests. I am a diverse and complex individual—influenced by both nature and nurture, as we all are. Why is it that, even as our society champions uniqueness, it seeks to lump the uniques together, to normalize? I say it's okay to be unique and just leave it at that.

3

SEXUALITY 101

AGES 13–14

MANY PEOPLE have fond memories of high school. I am not one of them. I'd loved elementary school—gotten along well with classmates and made good grades. I was even a Cub Scout. But falling down the hay chute seemed to mark the death of innocence and usher in a world of confusion. To make matters worse, something happened the summer before ninth grade that would change the way I viewed myself, and ultimately alter the course of my life.

It was a hot, cloudless day. I had a few rare hours without chores, so I made my escape to our tree house—a huge oak tree, haphazardly nailed with scraps of wood that formed a crude staircase. I climbed to the platform at the top and instantly felt a surge of joy. The tree house was one of my last strongholds of youth, a place where I could revisit my boyhood. It made the perfect lookout for whatever foe my imagination conjured up. I'd been victorious in every battle, subduing each bloodthirsty enemy that appeared over the ridge.

I hadn't realized that I should have been on guard for approaching friends as well.

My neighbor must have seen me running to the tree house that day. We'd never interacted much, mostly because he was several years older than I was. Gabe always sat in the highly coveted back seat of the school bus. Must have been either well-respected or intimidating to pull that off. In any case, I was shocked and confused when he climbed up, uninvited, and initiated a sexual encounter. I really don't remember much about it, other than the way I felt afterward—dirty.

This was my first sexual experience with a male (or anyone for that matter). The rejection I felt at home was offset by this opposite sense of being wanted, even though I felt sick about it. And the ensuing secrecy on both ends of the spectrum pushed me deeper into a lonely world of gray. This first season of abuse didn't last long, but it was enough to throw my desires into question. I never told anyone. How could I? What would they think of me? I was left feeling exposed and vulnerable, yet isolated.

Self-preservation instincts took over. I started building walls, cementing each layer of heaviness with a mixture of denial, lies, desire, guilt, and shame. Unfortunately, those walls wound up boxing me in, rather than protecting me from further harm.

And so, my high school years started off in disaster. I'd traded in my happily oblivious disposition for a decidedly self-conscious demeanor. I was petrified the first day. So big. So many students. The abuse had taken its toll, and I was extremely uncomfortable in my own skin. I assumed I wouldn't fit in—so I didn't fit in.

I started hanging out with a not-so-great crowd, trying on rebellion, which seemed an appropriate mask. The recurrent thoughts in my head said I was no good, so I decided to act the part. I was living moment to moment, and didn't give much weight to potential consequences. Dabbling in Marlboros behind school property quickly anchored a hook in my flesh for years to come. I thought smoking made me look so cool. Pretty sure I was wrong about that.

To make matters worse on the social front, I'd started gaining weight in all the wrong places. I had a ravenous appetite, but my family height gene hadn't kicked in yet, so I wound up short and round. While other boys were getting taller and looking manlier, all of my growth hormones seemed to have been rerouted to my enormous feet. The kids called me Baby Huey after a cartoon character—a giant-footed, big-bellied duck in a diaper. Not exactly the image I'd been going for.

It wasn't long before my troubles went beyond name-calling. A kid in English class started harassing me. Each day when the bell rang, he'd push his way in front of me and stick out his hand. His reputation and demeanor told me he meant business, so I gave him my lunch money. This went on for many months while teachers never seemed to notice. Yet again, I felt violated, not protected by adults, and unable to tell anyone.

One day, I got the courage to stand up to him and we ended up fighting in the hallway. Finally, a teacher intervened and pulled the bully off me. He took him to the principal's office and the guy never bothered me again. I wish I'd learned from this example that advocating for yourself and reaching out for help actually *could* make things better.

Along with this day-to-day drama, I had a seemingly constant undercurrent of sexual stirrings to contend with. Puberty was in full bloom, and I wasn't sure what to make of my feelings. I thought girls were pretty but didn't have much interest in dating them. I also found guys attractive but didn't know what that meant.

I very clearly remember the first time anyone called me gay. There was this football player that everyone thought was good-looking, myself included. Apparently, he thought so too. As we passed each other in the halls one day, he turned back and sneered at me.

"What are you looking at, faggot?"

The word *faggot* rang in my ears as if a grenade had exploded, leaving a question reverberating in its wake.

Did he know something I didn't?

I added this to the mounting evidence that something was different about me—and not different in a good way as far as I was concerned.

Though it had been a bumpy ride, I survived the school year and was looking forward to the reprieve summer promised. But when it finally arrived, the peace I'd hoped for didn't come with it—the summers of my youth seemed gone forever. Relentless secrets continued to haunt me and new ones were lurking around the corner.

The next predator showed up, this time an adult recruiter. Ray, the farmhand that had been there when Grandfather pushed me, began initiating sexual encounters. He was married with kids, so I wondered how he could do such a thing. I would see more than once in my life that a marriage license didn't necessarily stop someone from heeding the call of dark sexual desire.

Ray was an attractive man, one of the role models of my youth. My feelings about his advances were different than they had been with Gabe. It still felt wrong and dirty like before, but there were brief moments of pleasure too.

What did this mean? Why did this keep happening?

Once again, I assumed it was my fault and decided it must have something to do with me.

I still believed in God. Was all of this okay with him? Did he create me this way? If not, why hadn't he protected me?

My questions were exhausting and seemingly unanswerable. It felt much easier to go with the wild current that was sweeping me farther and farther away.

Farther from God. Farther from myself. I was becoming a walking caricature of the real me.

HINDSIGHT REVELATIONS: BORN GAY?

Homosexuality wasn't discussed much in the small community where I grew up. I'd thought "homo" was just a loose term guys threw around to insult other guys. I wasn't really sure what it meant, not fully. Yet somehow, the idea began to stick. Words can affect people subtly, without them ever knowing what's happening inside their souls. Agreements can be made without ever picking up a pen to sign your name to the contract.

I'd found myself thinking about men more and more which stirred up a hornet's nest of questions: Why did I feel attracted to men? What did this mean? Was I gay? Had I been born gay? Or was this a learned practice, initiated by abuse?

Abuse comes in various forms, affecting its victims deeply in ways that last long after the physical event. Sexual abuse pierced my flesh, creating a sense of bondage. This type of abuse carries another dimension of disturbance if victims experience curiosity or any hint of physical pleasure. Victims might conclude that they wanted it to happen. In same-sex situations, they might assume they're gay. That's how evil works: twisting truth, distorting reality, and exploiting doubts.

If you're looking for hard facts on the subject of sexual identity, I'm guessing you'll be hard-pressed to find any. I couldn't go to the doctor to take a blood test that would tell me whether I was gay. Neither doctors nor scientists have reached a consensus as to why some people lean toward a same-sex orientation. There's no evidence to pin it on a single catalyst, although many theories have been explored (genetic, hormonal, developmental, social, cultural influence, etc.).

It's a complex subject—and I'm *not* saying it's the same for everyone—but in my case, I'd never wondered about being gay until after the abuse began. My lack of healthy, affirming relationships with a strong male role model put me on a flimsy foundation. I yearned for approval from older men, and in a twisted way, the abuse gave that to me. All of this threw my sense of identity into a tailspin, leaving me disoriented and wide open to pick up whatever was put in front of me.

4

SAFE HOUSE

AGES 14–15

THE GULF continued to widen between farm life and my developing likes and interests. This added weight to my growing concern that I was somehow abnormal. The rest of my family seemed content, but farm living did not seem like the life for me.

I felt like a disappointment, so different from my dad. There would be no following in his footsteps—not by my feet anyway—no way I was taking over the family business. When I was young, the farm had seemed so vast that I couldn't explore every inch if I tried. But as a teen, it felt confining. Memories and secrets tormented me. I'd put so many walls up to protect myself that it began to feel like living in a maze. I longed for escape, but didn't know where to turn.

As it turned out, I didn't have to look far. Alice and Bob Henderson were family friends from church who seemed to intuitively understand my needs. Alice was full of energy and always one step ahead of everyone else. A former flight attendant, she stood out among the rural landscape as fascinatingly cosmopolitan with her amazing sense of fashion and stories of exotic travel. Alice and I bonded instantly over love of adventure and appreciation of beautiful things. I always said she was my second mom.

Alice and Bob made a striking couple. I was enamored with them. Bob worked on his family farm, but was very different from my dad—approachable and relaxed. I loved the smell of his cigar. He never quite became a father figure to me, but at least he was safe. Bob was a good guy and a great storyteller.

I was captivated by the way everything was decorated in the Henderson's modern home. But the thing I loved most about staying with them was that I felt free to be myself. I asked to go to their house whenever I could. I think my mom was jealous of my relationship with Alice sometimes, but she never really said so. Maybe she knew it was the escape I needed.

The Hendersons had two daughters who were a few years younger than I was. The girls and I would play games or watch TV sometimes, but Alice was the one I loved spending time with. I especially liked helping in the kitchen, something I wasn't allowed to do at my house (women's work). While we baked together, Alice and I would talk about the local goings-on, or she would tell me stories and ask about school. I could tell that she truly enjoyed spending time with me. It was refreshing to my soul.

There was something so different about this family. I felt a sense of security with them. Like I belonged. Alice and Bob treated me like the son they never had—I even had my own bedroom. Of course, I loved my own family. And though it didn't always feel like it, I knew they loved me too. Yet I couldn't help feeling that I fit in better with the Hendersons. They introduced me to lighthearted living where laughter was the norm and unconditional acceptance was a deeply ingrained value.

Being with them was like living out an alternate story line, and though dreamlike, this version had the ring of truth. I was simply and beautifully David, a beloved son with a future and a hope. I dreamed of having my own family like this someday, complete with a white picket fence and kids playing on a swing set.

Unfortunately, this vision wasn't yet strong enough to convince me that it was truly possible. When I wasn't with Alice and Bob, the picture quickly faded—like a Polaroid in reverse. The darkness flooded back in as my hope was overwhelmed by the onslaught of lies that felt easier to believe.

At the intersection of this safe house and life beyond, I stood at the first of many crossroads I'd face. I wanted to take the lighted path that I'd caught a glimpse of, but couldn't seem to find my way in everyday life.

HINDSIGHT REVELATIONS: BELONGING

I now think of my time with the Hendersons, particularly Alice, as a gift from God. It was a glimpse of what it feels like to belong, a ray of light, a promise of hope. I think God sends special people into all of our lives like this (and he sends us to be "Alices" for others in return). Alice saw something in me that others didn't. She looked *into* me, not merely at or past me.

Bob was great too, although I had trouble connecting with him on a deeper level. Male relationships were complicated for me. I didn't know how to relate to a man that communicated unconditional love. The culture I'd grown up in—where men felt unable to show their feelings, especially affection for other men—created unnecessary tension in this regard.

The sense of belonging I felt with the Hendersons allowed me to be part of something, yet still be uniquely myself. This is so important. My shame seemed to evaporate here. It was as if the past was erased from eternity. They could only see me for who I really was.

I didn't know it then, but this is a picture of what life with Jesus is like. This was a taste of my true identity—not the broken farm boy, nor the conglomerate personality I was beginning to try on at school and elsewhere.

I will always think of the Henderson's as my safe house. It was a place of peace and freedom that helped me shape my dreams. I'm forever grateful to Alice, and I try to create a similar welcoming atmosphere of belonging in my home today.

Although maybe not exactly in the way I thought, I did eventually see the dreams that were planted in my safe house come to fruition. But I chose the scenic route to realization, so we're not to that part of the story just yet.

5

MAGNETS

AGES 15–18

DO OPPOSITES ATTRACT? Or does like attract like? As I moved from puberty into adolescence, the subject of attraction became one huge distraction. Once you notice something, it can consume your focus, especially when you try to stop thinking about it.

As I continued to wonder what was going on with my body and desires, high school wasn't helping. Masculinity was the gold standard, just as it was on the farm. Jocks ruled. I didn't fit into that scene, so had to look elsewhere. I wasn't interested in having a girlfriend—the girls I knew only seemed friendly when I had cash in my pocket. Most of all, I desperately wanted a close friend. Enter Alex. He lived in a neighboring town, but we started hanging out on weekends sometimes. I envied his rugged good looks—tousled dark blond hair, steel-blue eyes, sinewy frame. He had a nonchalant, cool-guy charisma about him, like James Dean or the Marlboro Man. I quickly developed a case of hero worship, but we were just friends.

Alex and I were able to spend more time together over the summer of my sophomore year. I was even allowed to go stay with his family a handful of times. It was like entering a different world—an exhilarating escape from farm life.

His friendship started helping me feel more confident, at least in some respects. The fact that I'd finally started growing didn't hurt either. By August of that year, I'd topped off at six-two and leaned out considerably. I wore my bangs long, Beatles-style, and thought I was looking pretty hip. Even had leisure suits that would have made Elvis jealous. It was quite the transformation. In fact, I changed so much over the summer that classmates didn't recognize me when our junior year started.

I still made time to hang out with Alex when his dad let him borrow the car. Somewhere over the course of our friendship, we began "messing around." He admitted that he was sexually attracted to me, but insisted he wasn't gay. Alex had this way of sounding like he knew what he was talking about, so I went with it. I was attracted to him too and liked being with him. If Alex wasn't gay and we were doing the same things, maybe I wasn't gay either.

But I wondered why my scales of attraction seemed to tip toward men. I hadn't felt this way about a girl yet, so I had nothing to compare it to. I didn't know what to make of these feelings and couldn't ask anyone else about it. I was too ashamed to bring it up.

So I was on my own. Maybe Alex was right. Maybe this was just part of growing up.

HINDSIGHT REVELATIONS: NO SHAME IN ATTRACTION

If older me could talk to younger me, I'd tell him not to place so much weight on physical attraction—not to worry so much about what it means or doesn't mean. Today, I simply appreciate the beauty of the human form as a magnificent work of God. In the same way I might marvel at a majestic tiger or gorgeous sunset, I'm free to notice that a man is handsome (or a woman is lovely) without it meaning anything more. Feelings of attraction can be more complex than appreciation. But it's probably safe to assume that attraction isn't based on gender alone. As with sexual orientation, studies have been unable to pinpoint a single cause that determines attraction. To say that my attraction to men conclusively meant that I was homosexual (or bisexual) isn't any more true than saying that someone who likes the taste of wine is an alcoholic.

Desire does not define me. The enemy of my soul tries to use temptation against me, but it's how I respond that matters. What tempts me can actually offer insight. My desire was to feel loved by men. Attraction is not the same as love, so giving into temptation could never fill that desire. I needed to look deeper.

Beyond mere attraction, I now know that there's so much more to consider, much more than I was able to understand as an adolescent. Sex was created for a beautiful purpose, but like many things that are inherently good, it can be used in a way that was never intended. This affects not only the body but also the deepest part of the soul. A person's entire identity can begin to revolve around sexuality. Aren't we much more than this?

Sexual orientation proclamations are now being made as early as grade school, while even adults—including experts in the field—don't agree on what's normal or healthy in terms of development. I believe we have access to truth that we won't find through any scientific study. If we search our hearts, we can find it.

But instead, we often listen to the louder voice. Most of our worst decisions are driven by the desperate fear that we're worthless. This fear opens the door to shame, which only leads to deeper self-loathing. Shame tells us, "You're damaged goods, so you might as well…XYZ. It's the only thing that will make you feel better." Shame says, "You're abnormal, but here's a way for you to fit into a group with other misfits like you (at least you won't be alone)."

Shame is poisonous. But courage is the antidote. Thankfully, I've learned to fight back. I don't allow temptation and shame to define me, nor drive the way I think or act.

6

WHO CAN I TRUST?

AGES 18–21

PUTTING my trust in people started to seem like walking on a frozen pond. The more naive I was about surface conditions—not to mention what might lie underneath—the more dangerous it became. By my senior year of high school, I'd already stepped on thin ice one too many times. Cracks were showing up everywhere, making it difficult to find a safe place to step.

I decided my best bet was to find a new pond entirely. I'd been counting the days until graduation, hoping to start a new life at college. The town I was moving to wasn't particularly exciting, but at least I'd be a few hours away from the farm and anyone who knew me. As it turned out, I found the old adage to be true: you can't run from your problems. Well you *can*, but they tend to follow.

College ended up being much harder than expected. I'd never learned how to take notes or study, so I quickly found myself in over my head. Socially, I just exchanged one small town for another and didn't fit in any better here. My roommate grew marijuana in the back of the dorm building and offered me my first hit of weed. I wasn't impressed, so I didn't wind up with the stoner crowd.

I did make one new friend. Brad and I met in the student union and started eating lunch together. He was a Christian and talked about God sometimes. It didn't bother me, but didn't sway me either. I simply listened politely, the same way I'd gone to church politely to make my parents happy. I don't think Brad was trying to convert me or anything. He simply struck me as a nice guy being himself. Even though I had no interest in following God at the time, I found myself curiously drawn to people of faith. I thought there might be something to it, but decided it wasn't for me.

Brad and I didn't have much time to get to know each other since I only lasted one semester in college. With my apathetic attitude at the wheel, my grades quickly ended up in the ditch.

I was headed back to the farm.

Sitting in my childhood bedroom, I heard the familiar whispers of shame.

You're such a failure. Can't you do anything right? Now you're right back where you started. You'll probably live here forever.

Surprisingly, a stronger thought fought back this time.

I can't give up. I have to get off this farm.

Then and there, I decided there was no way I was staying. I went to the new mall in town and got my first paying job as a busboy, not knowing this would lead to more than eight years in the restaurant business. I borrowed $1,500 from my dad to buy a car—a black, 1967 two-door hardtop Cougar with baby blue leather bucket seats. Coolest car ever. It finally felt like freedom had arrived. I loved driving around with friends at night, hanging out at the drive-thru. Having a car gave me space to make some moves in other areas as well.

I decided to try dating a girl, so I asked a friend to set me up with someone. One night, I took her to the drive-in—but didn't watch the movie. This was my first sexual encounter with the opposite gender. I didn't think much of the experience itself, but thought I was finally doing what I was meant to do as a man. I would soon learn that my underwhelming feelings had less to do with her gender and more to do with a lack of chemistry or affection.

In fact, there was another girl I was about to meet that would elicit a very different response.

My new job had quickly become my life. I was promoted from busboy to waiter to manager in a matter of months. There were interesting people to meet and customers to make happy every day. I absolutely loved it. This is where I met Jill. We developed a playful friendship and would tease each other constantly. Eventually, we started dating.

I felt better than I had in a long time and was really enjoying life. Jill and I had great fun together. We even took a trip to Florida. When I saw the ocean for the first time, I couldn't get over how beautiful it was. The world suddenly seemed so big compared to the little farm life I'd known. I was overcome by a sense of freshness and adventure. I walked the beaches feeling connected to something on a grander scale, though I wasn't sure what. Later, I remember thinking if only we could have stayed in Florida, maybe everything would have been okay.

My feelings for Jill were difficult to sort out. I didn't really know what real love was, but I definitely cared about her and enjoyed being with her. She pursued me and that made me feel good. Sometimes it felt a little like playing house. I'd redirected my life toward this woman, but couldn't shake my attraction to men. I did my best to ignore this.

Jill was an only child, spoiled rotten by an overprotective mother who wanted whatever made her baby happy. As such, I'd always been welcomed as part of the family. They involved me in almost everything they did and our lives were becoming increasingly intertwined. So it came as a complete shock when Jill announced, out of nowhere, that she was going into the military. She said she was leaving in two weeks.

I pelted her with questions: "Why the sudden exit? What about me? What about us?"

She deflected my concerns with an indifferent shrug and dismissed me without further comment.

It was about to become glaringly clear that Jill did exactly what she wanted, when she wanted. She did not need my permission.

Right before Jill's sudden departure, I'd taken on a new position as chef at a private club. It was a high-stress job, and I was feeling overwhelmed on every side. I had no idea what was going on with Jill. Were we still a couple? I turned to Alex for consolation and my feelings for him resurfaced. We spent a lot of time together as I tried to keep my mind off Jill.

Two months later, Jill came home on leave. She called me at work and asked me to come over. Said she needed to tell me something. I was anxious to see her and hopefully get some answers. So I drove over as soon as I finished my shift at the club.

Walking up to Jill's house, I tried to swallow the uneasy lump in my throat but that only made my stomach queasy. I figured I was just nervous to see her after all this time. Her mother was at work, so it would be just the two of us. Jill had told me to come on in when I got there, so I opened the front door a crack and tentatively called out to her.

"Jill? It's me…"

"Down in a minute," she hollered. "Make yourself comfortable."

The chances of me feeling comfortable in this moment were slim, but I took a seat on the living room sofa and tried to assume a relaxed posture without much success.

After several minutes that seemed like hours, I heard her coming down the stairs and lifted my gaze in her direction. Jill turned the corner in a movement that seemed to take place in slow motion as her dark hair swung around like a girl on a shampoo commercial. Her smile broadened as she walked toward me with her hands hugging her stomach. She stood on her tiptoes to give me a quick kiss, then stepped back and assessed my demeanor with an impish look in her big, blue eyes.

"Guessss what?" she asked, raising her eyebrows to match the inflection of her voice.

I was pretty sure I already knew the answer, but reluctantly played along.

"Uh…what?"

She lifted up her hands, as if to reveal the surprise. "I'm pregnant!"

She seemed oddly playful about it, like she couldn't wait to see me freak out.

I did not disappoint. My eyes widened, and I began to hyperventilate. I tried taking a deep breath, reluctantly eyeing her stomach as if it were Medusa's head. She was already showing at two months. A flood of emotions and thoughts rushed through me and burst out as a rambling river of words.

"What? I'm going to be a dad? Are you kidding me? I'm only twenty-one. We're not even married. What will my family think? My friends—"

She put a finger to my mouth to cut me off. "Don't worry. I'm having an abortion."

My initial thought was, *Whoa okay…I guess that takes some pressure off.*

But in reality, the nightmare was just beginning.

Jill said she would see me in six weeks. She was going back to the military base, where she planned to have the abortion. At that time, I was mostly numb with fear and thought it was best to let her handle it the way she wanted. I wasn't processing the situation long-term, nor from a moral standpoint. I thought the abortion meant my life wouldn't be turned upside down (but realized later how wrong I was).

I didn't tell anyone except Alex. He asked how I felt about it. "Dunno," I said, "I guess it's the best thing to do."

Back then, the realities of abortion weren't fully exposed as they are today. I'd never seen pictures of fetuses moving around, alive inside the womb. Abortion had recently been legalized, so I thought it must be okay. Just making a problem disappear. But I have to take full responsibility for the decision because I didn't fight it. As with so many of my young decisions, I chose the path of least resistance.

When Jill came home on her next leave, she phoned saying she needed to see me. Dealing with Jill's drama was the last thing I wanted to do since it was an emotional time for me already. My grandfather was on his deathbed and everyone was on edge, but I knew I should be supportive and find out how she was feeling after the abortion. I said she could come out to the farm if she wanted.

I sat on the porch, watching anxiously as her car pulled up. When she got out, I couldn't believe what I was seeing. She was still pregnant—*more* pregnant!

She said the doctors had tried everything, but the baby wouldn't abort. So they were sending her to a navy hospital in Philadelphia to try an experimental technique. I nodded and we were both quiet for a while. I had no idea what to say or do about this, or whether Jill even wanted me to say or do anything. She'd made up her mind and never asked for my opinion or blessing.

So I changed the subject and told her what was going on with Grandfather. I shared the mixed emotions I felt, lamenting that our broken relationship was never going to be fixed. I was talking about Grandfather, but as the words came out, I realized the same was true about my relationship with Jill. I felt helpless and hopeless about both situations.

Grandfather died later that week. I was a pallbearer, along with my brothers and cousins. While we sat in the car waiting to go to the cemetery, I started crying. I wondered why I was the only guy crying. Grandfather had liked all of them. They had his blessing—shouldn't they be more upset than I was?

It would be many more years until I would fully understand those emotions. I wasn't mourning his death so much as I was grieving over the loss of any chance for healing or closure. Thankfully, I was wrong about this and eventually learned that the grave doesn't prevent forgiveness.

The following week, Jill's mother called, inviting me to be present for the abortion. We flew out to meet Jill at the hospital. When I walked into the room, she was lying in bed. I immediately noticed that her stomach was bloated to the size of a full-term pregnant woman. I was terrified. My emotions were on a rampage, and I didn't know where to put them. She explained that since the suction method hadn't worked, they were trying a new method that involved putting a long needle into her stomach and filling it with solution.

Some people in white coats took Jill to the operating room. I sat in the maternity ward waiting room feeling anxious, but not for the same reason as the other dads. I looked around in a daze. Expressions of joy were everywhere. Echoes of newborns crying, the sweet smell of new life—it was almost more than I could bear. *What was I doing? What was happening to Jill's baby…MY baby?*

But I couldn't think of it that way. I struggled to push down any feelings that something immoral might be taking place. Eventually, one of the white coats let us know that Jill was ready for visitors. Her mother said I could go in first.

I sat down beside Jill's bed. "You okay?" I asked.

Jill looked at me with the same mischievous smile she'd had when first telling me she was pregnant. She spoke with a strange sound of exhilaration coloring her voice.

"It felt like someone just flushed a toilet inside me and then…voilà, it was gone!"

Voilà?

It?

I stared at her in horror and disbelief. Something happened to me in that moment that I didn't understand. I had the sense that there was evil all around. It was similar to when I looked into my grandfather's eyes after he'd pushed me.

I suddenly realized I'd been acting the same way I'd behaved as an abused kid, just going along with whatever happened. Something inside me was revolting against this now, but it was too late.

A voice inside my head whispered, *You just killed your son.*

Guilt rushed in like floodwaters mixed with a deeper shame than I'd ever known. It polluted my mind as I was caught in its toxic undertow. I was overcome with grief. Worse, I knew it was all my fault.

What have I done?

In a state of wretched self-loathing, I sheepishly said goodbye to Jill, not knowing it would be the last time I would ever set eyes on her. We never talked again.

When I got home, I couldn't face the truth of what had just happened. I'd stepped on that dangerously familiar thin ice, and now it was breaking all around me. I couldn't take my actions back. I wished there was do-over, that someone had stopped me from allowing this to happen. But I hadn't reached out to anyone who might have helped.

I'd hoped that returning to work would take my mind off things, but coworkers kept asking what I'd been doing in Philadelphia. I lied, of course. It felt like the only option. This further burdened my soul as I tried to bear the weight of it alone. Struggling to come to terms with the abortion, I couldn't find a speck of relief in any sort of justification or atonement. So I resorted to my usual coping method: I buried it deep down in a chamber of my heart and locked the door. It was never to be opened, as far as I was concerned. Not by anyone. Not even God. After this unforgivable act, I was certain he'd condemn me to fire and brimstone.

I decided the best solution was to get on with my life. I considered dating another woman, but was gun-shy since my relationship with Jill had ended in disaster. What had felt good and safe? Only Alex. Was that the route to take? I had to get off the ice and find some stable ground. In my mind, Alex seemed like the only real option.

The road had been paved. It looked like the easiest path, so that's the one I took.

HINDSIGHT REVELATIONS:
THE PAIN OF ABORTION

We often champion "rights" in our society. Rights carry a sense of freedom and empowerment.

People say it's important to protect a woman's right to choose. But when we grant a woman her rights, do we deny the rights of the baby? Of the father? Of grandparents and relatives? Of people waiting years to adopt?

Whether it's legal or not, perhaps the real tragedy is that many people don't think it through. I didn't.

I was scared and didn't think about the reality of what was happening. I know now that the injection they used poisoned my baby and chemically burned him alive from the inside out. I've read that this method is still (although rarely) used for late-term abortions today. The baby may suffer for up to an hour before dying.

The realities are hard to discuss, but need to be known and taken into consideration. There are less-invasive methods, but the outcome is the same.

Just as I'd never thought through abortion, I'd never thought about the possible consequences of unprotected sex. By my teens and twenties, the "free love" culture had made its way across the United States and we were living out the sexual revolution. This was before AIDS had been identified as a threat, before "safe sex" was discussed. Throw Roe v. Wade into the mix, and you start to see hundreds of thousands of abortions each year.

Perhaps the tide is turning. After peaking in 1990, when more than 1,429,247 abortions were reported to the Centers for Disease Control (CDC), abortions appear to be on the decline. Authorities disagree as to the reason, some citing wider access to better birth control, others citing a shift in public opinion.

As people argue over choices and rights, I wonder if they weigh the great responsibility that comes along with a "right." Just because we may have the right to do something, it's not necessarily the right thing to do.

Dealing with the pain caused by abortion is a gut-wrenching and lifelong journey. Only by trusting that I am loved unconditionally by God, have I been able to experience healing and forgiveness—but it's a process. I can't change the past, I can only let the past change me.

I have three beautiful children now, which makes me realize what I've given up all the more in letting my unborn son die. I trust that I will meet him one day. I trust that God has somehow worked even this evil for good, in ways I can't begin to understand.

7

GETTING OUT
OF DODGE

EARLY TWENTIES

IN AN EFFORT to put the past behind me, I immersed myself in work. It wasn't long before I was hired as a chef at the busiest restaurant in town. The atmosphere excited me. With its close proximity to Pittsburgh, the restaurant was hopping with businesspeople and a sophisticated clientele that I found intriguing.

This was where I met Carson, who also intrigued me. He commanded the kitchen in a Gordon Ramsay kind of way and wasn't shy about letting the staff have it if they messed up. Thankfully, I managed to stay on his good side. After work, we would often go out for drinks and talk about life.

Carson's parents died young, so he'd been on his own for much of his life. Perhaps that's how he'd cultivated his dry wit and loner mystique. He was handsome by anyone's standards—tall and lean, with a striking combination of thick waves of black hair and catlike green eyes. In the early weeks of our friendship, I had no idea that Carson dated men. I only knew that I was undeniably drawn to him.

Meeting Carson changed my life forever. Our relationship eventually became sexual and I found myself surprised by a flood of emotions. I felt a deep love for him unlike anything I'd ever known. Up until now, I had never felt truly, demonstratively loved by a man—not by my father, nor grandfather. Could this person finally fill that hole in my heart? It seemed that he could. I was all in.

We tried to keep our relationship hidden from everyone. Even Alex. It was weird to keep a secret from him, but things were awkward between us. Alex had been dating someone seriously for a while now and he hardly ever came in town to see me. So Alex and I drifted apart. Carson and I, on the other hand, became inseparable. And people started noticing. A few coworkers saw right through our facade and teased us with knowing comments.

One weekend, Carson invited me on a trip to visit a friend in the city. This was the first time I met other men who lived openly gay, at least among themselves. Something told me this was where I belonged. They loved on me and made me feel special, the way my grandma used to. They told me how handsome I was and reaffirmed how much Carson adored me. I hadn't felt so accepted since my time with Alice and Bob. Entranced by the power and lofty emotions of romantic love, and thrilled to feel like part of a group culture—it was everything I'd longed for. (I would later learn that, unlike my sense of belonging at Alice and Bob's, there were strings attached to this group's acceptance.)

I never wanted that summer to end. It was my Cinderella story, admittedly with a bit of a twist. Autumn came, and Carson went back to finish his last year of college. He was two states away in Indiana and I missed him so much. Meanwhile, I kept working and eventually saved enough money to get my own apartment in town.

Freedom, here I come, I thought.

I was finally feeling like things were going well for me. I was happy. My parents, however, weren't quite as happy about my all-consuming "friendship" with Carson. Though we never discussed it, I'm sure they had concerns about what was going on in my life. Carson and I never displayed the romantic side of our relationship (outside our circle of friends). I doubt we were fooling anyone, but it seemed important to me to keep up the pretense.

I couldn't wait to see Carson on his next break. Winter weather and my job had conspired relentlessly to keep us apart. When spring finally arrived, offering hope of a reprieve, I faced new concerns. Carson would graduate in May and was looking for a job. What would happen to us? I had fallen madly in love. I had found someone I thought I could trust with my innermost thoughts, with my very heart. I truly thought I couldn't live without him.

As I worried about losing Carson, pesky questions consumed my thoughts.

What would happen if we broke up? Was I officially gay now? Or was I simply in love with a man? Was there a difference? What did God think about this?

I quickly pushed away this last concern by reasoning that God was way up in heaven—I wasn't dead yet, so I had time to work everything out with him later.

Before I could figure any of this out, Carson's job opportunity came knocking. When he told me he was moving to Chicago, my mind started reeling again.

He's leaving? What about me? How would I live without him? Carson smiled empathetically, seeing the panic on my face. "Come with me," he said. "Come to Chicago."

My heart flooded with relief and I immediately said yes. As I let the idea sink in, a new worry surfaced. How was I going to get out of Dodge without exposing our relationship?

The scheming began. I told my family and friends that I'd gotten a job in Chicago, and "my good buddy" Carson just so happened to be moving there too. It's comical to assume that anyone bought this, but I thought I was so clever. Alex definitely wasn't fooled. He'd never liked Carson and was furious with me when I shared the news. I wrote Alex off as jealous and selfish, thinking he didn't really care about my happiness. I didn't need his blessing anyway. I had Carson now.

As August gave way to September, the move to Chicago was quickly approaching. My mother planned a going-away party with friends and family. Everyone and everything was right on track, just like I'd planned. Carson was going to move ahead of me and find an apartment for us, then I would find a job when I got there—surely that would be no problem. But all of my careful planning was about to be unraveled by a single phone call from Carson.

"David?" I could tell something was off by the tone of his voice. "I need to tell you something." There was an excruciatingly long pause. "I got a better position, an amazing job offer in Indianapolis…so I took it."

The weight of my heart sinking made it difficult to stand. A wave of dread washed over me, no doubt erasing all color from my face. It was the feeling of being caught in a lie, even though I hadn't technically been caught yet.

"But I've told everyone I had a job in Chicago," I reminded him. He didn't seem to see the issue.

"Don't worry, you can come to Indianapolis," he reassured me. Sure, that was an easy for solution for him. Was I supposed to just drop everything and follow him—wherever *he* decided? No discussion? I had no say? His take-it-or-leave-it attitude exasperated me. Thoughts thrashed around my head in a panicked frenzy. *How was I going to explain this to my family? "Guess what? I just happened to fall into a job in*

Chicago the same time as Carson, but now we're both coinciden-tally moving to Indianapolis instead. Crazy, right?"

My hidden life might be exposed. I wasn't ready for that. Worse still, Carson didn't seem to care. This was a glimpse of the Carson I would come to know. If I hadn't been blinded by heady love and my first tastes of happiness in a very long time, I might have noticed that it was always all about him. But at that time, I couldn't imagine life without Carson. I decided it was worth the risk to rearrange everything for him, even if it meant being discovered. Thankfully, before I had to explain this new development the most amazing thing happened. Unprompted by me, the restaurant I was working for asked if I would transfer to fill a vacant position—at its *Indianapolis* franchise. I couldn't believe it!

Did the corporate office somehow know what was going on? Did God in heaven still hear my cries?

It really did seem like a miracle. I didn't have to lie any-more; this was legit. Now my family wouldn't question any-thing. At least, that's what I told myself.

Carson moved to Indy ahead of me and my going-away party took place as scheduled. My little secret seemed to be just fine. I decided it was best not to mention that he was moving to Indy too, so I wrote him out of the picture as far as my family knew. I emptied my apartment into a U-Haul and spent my last night at the farm. I was so proud of how I'd hidden everything. I felt like I'd gotten away with something. But was I only fooling myself?

As I climbed up into the moving truck, Mother stood crying while Dad did his best to comfort her. My emotions welled up for the first time. I wondered why I was crying. Was it because my mother was upset or was there something more? Mom had always said I could be whatever I wanted to be—doctor, cowboy, whatever. What would she think about me moving off to live romantically with another man? In today's culture, this has become more accepted but things were not as open then. What I was doing would have been scandalous. Whether or not my family suspected what was really going on, talking about it was the last thing any of us wanted to do.

I steadied myself long enough to drive out of sight and finally get away from the farm for good. This had been my dream for so long. But as I exited on to I-70 and started heading west, I sobbed as I passed all the familiar exits. I wasn't sad to leave, yet these were not tears of joy either.

Perhaps I was experiencing the sorrow of conviction, as I somehow sensed I was driving further down a road that grieved my soul. Even as I pursued my dreams of a new life where nothing would get in the way of my choices, I doubted the wisdom of those choices. But I quickly pushed those doubts away with thoughts of Carson, and love, and the excitement of living in a city.

Ready or not…Indiana, here I come.

HINDSIGHT REVELATIONS:
THE PARENT TRAP

It's easy to think if only such and such had happened (or hadn't happened), things could have been so different. It's also tempting to pass the blame.

Do I wish sometimes that my parents had intervened (assuming they knew what was going on)? Maybe, but I don't know if it would have mattered. I loved that my mother was always so unconditionally supportive. As a parent, I know how hard it is. Each kid is different. I've known people whose parents totally severed contact with them over lifestyle choices, perhaps out of embarrassment or hoping it would be a catalyst for change. The pain on both sides breaks my heart. Whether parents are lenient or strict, this doesn't guarantee a certain result. There are no formulas for perfect parenting.

I'm extremely grateful that I maintained my relationship with my parents. In spite of any differences of opinion, and even if we had to sweep a few things under the rug, I always knew they loved me. I'm not advocating dishonesty—I wish I'd felt more comfortable talking to my parents. But I can't imagine not having had them in my life because of my choices.

Sometimes love agrees to disagree.

I believe several things in my life stacked up to point me toward the road I eventually chose. I can't say that things would have played out any differently if my parents had tried to convince me to choose a different path. I might have run that much farther, that much faster, who knows?

Because I attributed the way I saw my father and grandfather to the way I saw God, I thought he was distant and uninterested at best, or angry and vengeful at worst. If I had known God as a loving father, I might have seen the beautiful truth. How he laid out boundaries that were in my best interest. How he gave me the freedom to choose. When I chose wisely, he celebrated with me. And when I chose poorly, he wept over me. His love for me has never changed.

I try to follow this example with my own kids. I hope that they know they can come to me with anything, that I will do my best to offer wise counsel (even if it's not what they want to hear), and that I will always love them—no matter what.

8

EMBRACING THE LIFESTYLE

MID-TWENTIES

THE SIX-HOUR DRIVE to my new home gave me plenty of time to settle my emotions. When I crossed the border into Indiana, I smiled at the sign that read, "Welcome to Indiana, Crossroads of America." They must have put that sign there just for me—I definitely was at a crossroads.

Nearly everything that happened in my life seemed to be leading me down this path. And now, I'd made the choice to see where it led. I was embracing a new life—more to the point, a new lifestyle. My mother's words came back to me: I could be whatever I wanted to be. Since I no longer wanted to be a cowboy, it was time to try something else on for size. I rolled down the window and took a deep breath. It was as though I'd never breathed air before. Everything felt different and alive with possibility.

Carson had rented a townhouse in a suburb called Carmel. We lived on the new, posh side of town, just about thirty minutes north of Indianapolis. It was amazing. We're talking the epitome of late-seventies chic, which would not be complete without wall-to-wall avocado green carpeting and harvest gold appliances. A sliding glass door opened to a porch overlooking a serene pond, complete with lovely geese.

I thought I'd arrived in heaven. (I would come back down to earth soon enough. The geese I had initially found so charming could be quite mean and vile—and they weren't the only ones.)

For the moment, everything seemed perfect. It felt like spring more than fall; newness was everywhere I looked—new surroundings, new job, new love. I felt born again, though not in a spiritual sense. I couldn't have been more excited. Other than Carson, no one knew me here. I could live how I wanted to. No barriers. No one looking.

For the first time in a long time, I didn't feel like a victim. In fact, I felt invincible.

Carson had already started working and seemed happy in his new position. I didn't have to start my job for a few weeks, so I used the time to furnish our home. I enjoyed being creative and was able to stretch what little money we had to make everything feel cool yet homey. I was like a kid on Christmas vacation, when reality is suspended and all seems right in the world. In a blink, the clock started ticking again and demanded that I reengage in real life.

My new job was at a beautiful lakeside restaurant. It was so massive that they needed two kitchens to keep up with all the orders when the tables were full. I was immediately overwhelmed by the workload and underwhelmed by my lack of rapport with the staff. My insecurities puffed up, leaving my hope deflated.

I was dismayed to learn that cities could be just as isolating as small towns. The clean slate I'd been enjoying in my personal life didn't work in my favor here. I was just another number to this restaurant, an outsider starting over again—without the respect I'd earned at my previous job. The half-hour drive in traffic there and back fueled my frustration. I would count the minutes until my shift was over so I could get home to Carson, where I felt loved and supported.

Life struck a best-of-times/worst-of-times balance: I loathed work, but loved everything else. I fully immersed myself in the gay lifestyle. It was amazing to discover that a whole other world existed. While I'd been growing up and feeling so confused, alone, and different, an entire culture built around gay men had been making its way from the West Coast to Middle America. Weekends felt like a fantasy life, a whirlwind of flamboyance where I was no longer alone in my appreciation of fashion, beauty, style, and hot music.

We partied—a lot. A typical weekend night started at ten o'clock with laughing it up at the comedy club or applauding the drag queens. There were two gay bars in town. We'd dubbed the first one "Ye Olde Faggot Bar." It was dark and subdued, mostly frequented by the "old queers," as we playfully called them. On the other side of the spectrum was the "Fun Bar," where the beautiful young men flocked and the dancing never stopped. There was always a packed house and plenty of booze, drugs, and poppers (an inhalant, common to the seventies disco scene). It was nothing to close the club down at three in the morning and then go out to breakfast with a fascinating assortment of people.

As our circle of gay friends grew, this became the norm. I seemed to fit right in and didn't have to pretend anymore. My new identity, at least in my eyes, had become "the blond guy with the studly boyfriend that everyone else wanted." Yet even as I enjoyed this sense of peer acceptance, I quickly learned that behind the facade of friendship lurked a layer of sexual hunting. True or lasting monogamy was rare.

Monday morning would always come too quickly. I would drag myself through work then settle into my role as a partner at home. We lived like a newly married couple.

Carson would arrive home around 4:30 p.m. and I'd get in an hour or two later. I'd fix dinner and he would help clean up. It was the All-American dream, as far as I was concerned. We would snuggle up and watch our favorite show, *Dallas*. I even bought the same abstract couch they had on the show (which I thought was the coolest thing ever). My life was becoming everything I'd hoped for.

Winter arrived and I was excited to spend my first Christmas at home with Carson. As I started making plans, I hit a snag—my family expected me to come to the farm. The holidays turned out to be a showcase of lies. I lied to my parents about when I could come visit, arranging it so I wouldn't have to spend much time with them. I lied about who I lived with and what I did for fun. I lied about how well I was doing at work. I tried to make it look like the farm boy went out and done good, manipulating the truth in the eyes of everyone, even myself.

Deep in my soul, there was a longing to be free from hiding. If I had to hide who I was, what did that mean? I was happy with Carson, but was this the real me? Keeping secrets and wearing masks had become such a part of my life from early on that it was often hard to distinguish lies from truth.

The winter passed uneventfully, gradually melting into the warm blush of spring. One Sunday morning, Carson and I went out for brunch—Carson loved sipping champagne before noon then coming home for an afternoon nap. While he slept, I turned on the TV to unwind for a bit until he woke up and changed the channel to a religious station. He made fun of everyone on the show and any loser that would actually "fall for that stuff."

Carson didn't believe in God and thought people who did were weak. His childhood had hardened him in many ways. After his parents died, Carson wound up bouncing around in the foster system. I could sometimes see his dark pain rise to the surface. Perhaps this fueled his disdain for anything God-related. I had the opposite core response, so it always bothered me when he would voice his contempt. I figured it wasn't worth an argument, so tried to dismiss it.

It wasn't hard to ignore him this particular day since my mind was preoccupied with something else. The new restaurant we tried for brunch had really appealed to me. It was so fun and happening. The wait staff wore bold red-and-white-striped shirts, along with crazy hats in various styles. Carson encouraged me to apply for a position and I did so first thing Monday morning. The manager called me that evening to schedule an interview. Carson seemed really happy about this, and I was always striving to please him.

The following morning, I found myself sitting in the empty restaurant with a cup of coffee talking with the head manager. He was impressed by my résumé and asked what part of the house I would like to manage. Out of nowhere, I heard myself say I wanted to be a waiter. *Um, what?* For one thing, this seemed like a step back in my career. For another, I had very little experience waiting tables. I must have really liked those uniforms and hats. The manager looked at me quizzically then shrugged his shoulders and told me I could start anytime. I gave notice to my other employer, which felt like the longest two weeks of my life.

Finally, my first day at the new job arrived. During training, I was surprised by the strict procedures they used. They weren't messing around. But it was a work-hard/play-hard mentality and we actually had a lot of fun. I was enamored with the whole environment. Everyone seemed to like me, which was a nice change of pace from my previous job.

I worked hard but loved serving people, so it didn't feel like work to me. I started on day shifts, then moved to nights, and quickly became one of the top ten waiters of the nationwide chain. The money started rolling in and I was soon making more than I had in management.

Our restaurant was *the* place to be, with people willing to wait as long as three hours for a table on weekends. I made new friends, both straight and gay. There was a culture of acceptance here; it was the first place I'd worked where people were openly gay. Didn't seemed to matter, as long as you didn't hit on the straight guys.

For a brief while, everything seemed to be coming back together—work, home, love life. Unfortunately, working nights meant getting home after Carson was in bed, which meant we weren't crossing paths much. I'd try calling him from the restaurant only to discover that he was rarely home. When I would ask where he'd been, the dismissive answer was usually, "Out with a friend." The hint of annoyance in his voice told me to stop asking questions.

I should have suspected something, but I didn't want to admit that my perfect world may not be so perfect after all.

As often as I tried to avoid it, the truth usually caught up with me (and sometimes smacked me dead in the face). My wake-up call came on a rare weekend off. A group of us was heading to Chicago to see the Village People and Donna Summer. The small-town boy in me was beside himself with anticipation to visit the Windy City and see my first big concert.

Had I known what that weekend had in store, I probably would have stayed home, opting to stay happily oblivious for as long as possible.

HINDSIGHT REVELATIONS:
HAPPINESS VS. JOY

If my life story was made into a movie, the screenwriter could take a few chapters out of context and come up with a completely different interpretation than if it was viewed as a whole. For instance, the past couple of chapters could have been sewn together with some jokes and a musical montage to create a romantic comedy—as long as it ended on the part where it looked like we'd live happily ever after. (Ever notice that romantic comedies don't usually have sequels?)

In some ways, I was living as a character in one of those movies. I was playing a role. Trying gay on for size. Admittedly, it seemed to fit pretty well. But not in the areas that mattered most, as I would soon learn.

Many people use what I call The Happiness Defense to justify their choices, or the choices of others. It's very American, after all. Built into our Declaration of Independence, the pursuit of happiness is identified as one of our unalienable rights. The rationale goes something like this: "Who cares—as long as I'm happy," or "What difference does it make—as long as they're happy." The key words to notice are "as long as." The problem with chasing happiness as a primary motivation is that it's a feeling, an emotion based on circumstances. Change the circumstances and your happiness can take a nosedive.

I've seen plenty of happiness come and go—regardless of relationships (and regardless of my partner's gender). Instead of chasing after fleeting happiness, I now look for joy. Joy isn't based on external circumstances. It's spiritual. It's deeper, truer. Surprisingly, you can be filled with joy even if you're not happy. But at this point in my life, I didn't know there was a difference between the two.

9

AN UNEXPECTED TWIST

MID-TWENTIES

I WOKE UP with the worst hangover I'd ever had. All I could remember from the night before was "YMCA" booming throughout the concert hall and somebody joking about the way Donna Summer was groping the microphone.

But I knew something else had happened. It was something important that I couldn't quite remember—or didn't want to. As my fog began to clear, I got sick all over again remembering what Carson had told me last night.

Right in the middle of my favorite song, he'd leaned in close and pointed to one of our friends, inadvertently spilling his cocktail on my shoe. If this wasn't enough to catch me off guard, what came next sent me over the edge.

"I slept with him," he said too loudly, speaking over the music with a slur. His demeanor was proud, not confessional—a rooster in a henhouse, bragging about his latest conquest.

I was too shocked to respond. A grenade had gone off and everything in the background faded away. I remained in a hazy stupor for the rest of the night and couldn't wait to get back to our friend's apartment. All I wanted was to go to sleep and exchange this nightmare for happier dreams.

Judging by the light outside now, I assumed it was late morning. It's not always true that everything looks better in the morning. To my bloodshot eyes, everything looked worse. Sure felt worse. I was raw with pain. The safe place I thought I'd found with Carson had been a lie. I'd been betrayed again. Hurt by Jill, hurt by Carson—apparently, gender made no difference. My world, my conception of the ultimate, happily-ever-after marriage seemed to be shattering before my eyes. I couldn't stop the feeling of loss from flooding every corner of my mind.

Carson appeared in the doorway, interrupting my apocalyptic thoughts.

"You up, David?"

I didn't respond right away. There was no way I could look at him.

"Where have you been?" I finally managed.

"I got up early and went to breakfast with the guys," he said. "Thought I'd let you get your beauty rest."

I would usually have found a comment like this endearing. Not today. I said nothing. Carson didn't catch my frosty mood, or more likely, tried to gloss over it.

"'Tis time we head out for Indianapolis, my pet," he said with a flourish in a bad Renaissance accent.

I bristled. His Prince-Charming moves that once made me swoon were now having quite the opposite effect.

The drive home seemed excruciatingly long. It was just the two of us and I didn't feel like talking. I decided to take a nap, hoping it would both cure my hangover and provide an escape from reality. When I opened my eyes, the sun was going down. We were almost home before I broke my silence.

"So...do you not love me?" I asked.

He assured me that he did. He promised never to cheat again. I wanted so much to believe him, so I decided to stay with him. In time, I would realize that Carson was indeed a leopard—his spots were there to stay.

Going back to life as usual wasn't as easy. The restaurant business was taking its toll on me. After the crew and I closed up the bar, I would often get home just as the birds were wishing me good morning with sweet songs that grated on my tired nerves. Each day blended into the next, creating a colorless streak of gray. I started questioning my relationship with Carson and my job too. Did I really want to do this all my life? Everything that had made me so happy just months ago now seemed tarnished.

Weekends came and went. We hit the bars as usual, but it wasn't the same. Carson and I had been together four years, and all that time I'd had eyes for no one else. However, after his "confession," I now found myself flirting with other guys. Nothing ever came of it, but this was a sure sign to me that our relationship was in trouble. I didn't believe Carson truly loved me, in spite of his constant attempts at reassurance. I questioned our future—couldn't seem to forgive and forget. Plain and simple, I no longer trusted him.

Thankfully, I'd found a trusted confidant in a dear friend at the restaurant. Emma was a blue-eyed, strawberry blond beauty, with a few light freckles dotting her nose and cheeks. Emma and I would share dreams of where we wanted to be when we got older. She couldn't wait to be married and dreamed of being a mother.

I didn't say so, but her dream always made me a little sad—it sounded so beautiful, but out of reach for me. At this time, gay couples weren't getting married and adopting children, so none of that seemed within my realm of possibility. Yet the idea of having a family stirred something deep within me. Could I have had that with Jill? Could I still have that?

Not with Carson. Even if it were possible for us to get married and have kids, I doubted that he would be interested.

My restlessness was becoming stronger. Sometimes I would try to talk about it with Carson, but that would only make things worse—I could tell he was bored by the conversation. I was almost twenty-five and didn't know what I wanted to do with my life. Restaurant life didn't feel sustainable. My relationship didn't seem sustainable. I had nothing to show for my investment in either of these pursuits.

I called Mom to see if she had any ideas on the job front. She asked if I wanted to go back to college, but I definitely didn't have that on my radar. At least I knew what I *didn't* want to do.

One morning, Emma and I were chatting between sips of coffee before the restaurant opened.

"Why don't you go to school to become a hairdresser?" she suggested. "You're handsome—I bet women would flock to you to have their hair done."

"I've never picked up a pair of shears in my life," I said, quickly dismissing the idea. "And anyway, how would I pay for school? I think it's pretty expensive."

But then I was quiet for a long while and Emma smiled a knowing smile, raising her eyebrows playfully. I gave her a light push as a non-verbal cue to "stop it" and she left me to my thoughts.

Hairdresser? Nah, that's crazy.

Crazy or not, the next day I found myself standing in front of a beauty school, arguing with myself about going in. I'd honestly never considered this as a career until Emma mentioned it, but now I couldn't get the thought out of my head. Somehow, it fit. On the other hand, I had zero experience. And what would my family think?

Finally I decided, *What the heck, why not?*

So I went in and asked about the program, holding my breath until the cost was revealed. Three thousand dollars for an eighteen-month program. That was definitely more money than I had. I sighed, a bit deflated.

"Ever done hair?" the lady asked. "No, never," I admitted.

"Well, that's no problem, kid. You look teachable enough," she said, laughing a hearty laugh. "I'll put in a good word for you with your instructor...who is me, by the way." She said this with a friendly wink, adding that I could start next week.

I told her I'd think about it. I really liked this lady. I really liked this idea. I saw hope peeking its head over the horizon again. Now, I just had to figure out the money thing.

That evening, I talked to Carson. He was on board—if I could figure out a way to pay for it and still contribute to our expenses. I called Emma, gushing with excitement and she gushed back.

"I just feel this is what God made you to do," she said.

I was intrigued by her comment. No one had ever said anything like this to me, especially not in relation to God. I'd not thought much about him for a long time, especially not as someone who might have something *good* planned for me. Yet something about her words rang true.

The next call I made was to Mom.

"I want to go to beauty school," I said. The line was silent for a moment.

"And how did you come to that decision?" she asked. It was my turn to pause. I didn't have a good answer.

"I'm really not sure, but you think I could borrow three Gs?"

"You need to ask your dad," she said.

Classic parenting move.

"Okay, I'll call back tonight when he gets home from the barn." I was nervous about asking Dad, but didn't have any other options. Thankfully, Mom had already briefed him, so it ended up being a quick conversation. He agreed to give me the money on the condition that I pay it back on a monthly basis. I detected something in his voice I couldn't put my finger on—sadness, resignation? I wouldn't find out until later that my decision to attend beauty school had confirmed their suspicions about my lifestyle. No one in our community back home was told that I'd entered the beauty industry.

Despite my family's lackluster enthusiasm for this idea, I was over the moon with excitement. I rearranged my schedule at the restaurant so I could go to school *and* pay for school, along with my other expenses. I worked five nights a week at the restaurant, but avoided the closing shift so I would still be awake enough to attend school four days a week.

On my first day, I arrived in a white shirt and black pants, as requested. My first instructor, Mrs. Thompson, pointed me to a kit with rollers, shears, and brushes. She was nowhere near as nice as the lady I'd met on my first day. Her demeanor was an odd mix of military leader and someone who didn't give a crap. She didn't even bother to get up. Just sat there, filing her nails while barking orders at me. She even called me by my last name.

"Okay, Lowry. You'll have to go in the corner back there, grab a mannequin, and start setting the hair," she said. "Do three hundred and we'll see if I let you out of the corner."

Three hundred? Three hundred what—push-ups? I wondered sarcastically.

I queried one of the other "cadets" and found out that Mrs. Thompson was talking about pin curls, so I got to work. I was less than thrilled with my first task, but figured this was just some sort of initiation ritual. As long as she didn't bring out tar and feathers, I'd stick around.

It didn't help that I was the only guy in the place. Mrs. Thompson didn't seem to like having a man on her turf.

What have you gotten yourself into, Lowry?

The other girls were a lot nicer to me. My station was right next to the breakroom, so I would talk to them as they went on break. Or sometimes they would come over and sneak a chat when Mrs. Thompson wasn't looking.

Overall, day one was not stellar. I never got the hang of pin curling, so I was worried that I may have to stay in that corner for the whole eighteen months. But thankfully, day two started off much better. My beacon of hope appeared around the corner and brought a flood of warm sunshine into the room with her.

"Well, hello, kid! I remember you."

I beamed back at this lovely woman with salt-and-pepper hair, just so, and a generous smile that was set off by crimson lipstick. She wore a vibrant, multi-colored pashmina that matched her personality.

"Call me Ms. Ruth," she said. "I'll be helping you learn the trade."

I was so relieved that Drill Sergeant Thompson wasn't my only teacher. I'd been wrestling with my mannequin's hair for an eternity and still didn't have a clue as to what I was really supposed to be doing. The mannequin started to look like a wild-haired Dolly Parton, so that's what I named her. At least I could find some humor in the situation.

After another heated battle with Dolly's mane, I was more than ready for a break. The girls and I headed to the lunchroom and I lit up my long-awaited Marlboro. (Yep, we smoked right there in the school. Times have changed.) The door opened and Ms. Ruth walked in, bringing that lovely glow with her.

What was it about this woman?

"Mind if I sit down with you?" she asked, lighting up a Virginia Slims. I scooted over to make room for her. "So tell me…how did you decide to do hair?"

"I don't know exactly," I said. "It all happened pretty fast." *Like a lot of other things in my life,* I thought, but didn't say. "My friend thinks this is what I was meant to do, but I don't know," I confided. "It feels like I just showed up here out of nowhere. I have no idea what I'm doing."

"Ah, I see," she smiled. "You know, kid, Jesus has a plan for all of us."

Jesus? The one on the cross from Sunday school? What does he have to do with my lack of ability to roll a proper pin curl?

I put my cigarette out, suddenly anxious to get back to my station. Ms. Ruth put her hand gently on my arm as I started to stand up.

"You need any help, just let me know, okay?" she said.

Help? Yes, help would be good.

It suddenly felt like my inability to tame Dolly's hair was a metaphor for my life. I really could use some help.

"Well, if you could show me how to put these pin curls in, that would be great."

"Sounds like a good place to start," she chuckled. "It's easy once you get the hang of it."

She followed me to my station.

"Let's see, I'm just going to get behind you now. My right hand will guide you…"

As Ms. Ruth came along side me, I experienced a feeling of warmth as she took my hands in hers. It was almost heavenly—a current of energy seemed to flow from her, leaving me with a profound sense of peace. I'd never felt anything like it.

Together, we put in a near-perfect pin curl.

"There you go, kid," she said, giving my hands a quick squeeze before letting go. "See, that wasn't so hard. You just keep practicing—you're going to be great."

I left that day with a new sense of worth, as though I'd found a missing piece of myself. I really saw myself becoming a hairdresser. But there was something else too. Something new stirring inside me. I was a little curious (and a little scared) to find out what it was all about.

HINDSIGHT REVELATIONS: PROVIDENCE AND TRANSFORMATION

Carson's betrayal was another pivotal event in my life. It was one of the worst things I could imagine happening at that time—but today I see it as a blessing. I'd convinced myself that a gay lifestyle was the answer, a way for me to find the love and acceptance I craved. I'd created a fantasy world that revolved around whatever made me feel *happiest in the moment*, assuming this was the same as *happily ever after.*

Infidelity shattered that illusion. It brought me back to reality and pointed me toward the road I was meant to travel. Carson, and the life I'd built around him, was a detour.

People often say they want to find God's will for their lives. We worry about finding the right spouse or perfect career. Those things are important, but what if the bigger picture is more important than the details? What if it's more about what God is doing in our hearts than what we're doing every little step of the way?

What if life is primarily about our transformation?

I'm not saying there's no such thing as a bad decision and there aren't consequences (both natural and spiritual) for our choices. I'm suggesting that God always finds a way, *in spite* of our choices. He can even use the resulting fallout to nudge us closer to where we're meant to be.

At ground level, my journey often looked like a zigzag trek in the wrong directions. But if you had a ten-thousand-foot view of my life, you could see the progression. You would see that it wasn't just a looping roller-coaster of valleys and hills, but also a gradual climb up a larger mountain. There may have been twists and turns, low points and plateaus, but God was always leading me upward.

I now recognize a consistent force that seemed to keep nudging me back in the right direction, regardless of my choices (which had largely been driven by circumstance and emotion). In the same way that Ms. Ruth had guided me to get the pin curl right, God's right hand had been guiding my life all along. I just didn't know it yet.

I'd decided long ago that God wasn't happy with me, probably even angry. But Jesus? I hadn't thought much about him for years—not until Ms. Ruth mentioned him. He'd always seemed friendly enough in the Bible stories of my childhood. The mention of his name initially made me feel uncomfortable. At the same time, I clearly remember being very intrigued.

10

A SNAKE OR A TREASURE?

MID-TWENTIES

IN THE DAYS that followed my interaction with Ms. Ruth, I felt a renewed sense of hope and excitement, as though I were on the cusp of something wonderful. Juggling both work and school was an adjustment for sure, but I eventually got used to my new schedule.

School was the hardest part because it was all so foreign to me. But I was starting to make friends with the other students, which helped a lot. Ms. Ruth continued to help too, as well as intrigue me with conversations about her "friend" Jesus—who was unlike any version of Jesus I'd ever heard about. She seemed to think he was right there beside her and she could just talk to him at any given time (which she often did). I thought it was sweet, but chalked it up as nonsense.

I believed in God and was okay with Jesus as part of that package deal, though I never really understood the whole God-as-man thing. Regardless, Jesus was in heaven—not on earth. My boiled-down version of "religion" went something like this: Step 1: Do your best to be a good person while on earth. Step 2: Go to heaven when you die. It was all very separate to me. I'd never recognized God's activity in my daily life, so honestly, I thought Ms. Ruth was a little nuts. Adorably fascinating, but nuts.

One day, some of us were gossiping in the breakroom about Ms. Ruth's infatuation with Jesus. We imitated how she said his name dripping with love, the way a teenage girl says the name of her new boyfriend. I made an offhand comment about the Bible being irrelevant today that seemed to trigger a fellow student. Debbie was a caramel-blond beauty with an intense, but welcoming personality. Her hazel eyes looked right into mine and issued a challenge: "Have you even read the Bible?"

"Uh…no, not really," I admitted, a little shocked that she was calling me out. Even though I'd grown up in the church, I'd never actually read the Bible. I'd always meant to read it as an adult, mostly as an intellectual pursuit. Sure would have come in handy in a case like this.

"Well, maybe you shouldn't make assumptions about something you've never read," she suggested.

I was embarrassed and didn't really have a rebuttal. So we just left it at that and went back to our stations.

Whether or not she knew that I'd been poking fun at her, Ms. Ruth continued to grace me with special attention and assistance. We began developing a relationship that went beyond the typical student-teacher paradigm. She would ask me about growing up on the farm, what my family life was like, etc. Interestingly, she never once asked what I'd been up to over the weekend, or about my "roommate." (I wasn't open about my sexuality at school, but I'm guessing people had a hunch.)

I told Ms. Ruth the stuff I thought was safe to share. She was easy to talk to, so I found myself opening up more than usual. I couldn't put my finger on what it was about her, but I was drawn to her. I felt like I could probably tell her anything and she wouldn't judge me. But for now, I kept my guard up. Not to mention, I'd buried much of my pain so deeply that I barely acknowledged it myself.

Outside of school, life continued on a pretty even keel. The restaurant was always busy on the weekends, but I would try to get out early so I could hit the bars downtown with Carson. We didn't talk much beyond saying hello and goodbye these days, so I was a bit surprised when he initiated an actual conversation with me on the way to the bar.

"How's school going for you?" he asked.

"Great," I said, "but my schedule is still wrecking me."

He nodded then paused. Silences hadn't usually been awkward between us, but this one was. I couldn't think of anything else to say. After a few moments, he spoke again.

"Have you met anybody?"

I wasn't sure where he was going with this.

"Well, I'm the only guy there. The rest are women," I reassured him.

Was that what he was fishing for? Reassurance? I couldn't tell, but he changed the subject just as quickly as he'd brought it up.

"What about your teachers?"

"They're mostly okay," I said. "There's this one, Ms. Ruth—she's got it going on, as far as I'm concerned. She's kind of a kook sometimes, but I've grown to like it. She talks to Jesus like he's a real live guy standing right next to her."

I laughed affectionately, picturing Ms. Ruth having a conversation with her invisible friend.

"Weird," Carson said, screwing up his face. He obviously was not as endeared by Ms. Ruth's eccentricity as I was. "You're kidding, right?"

"No, not a bit," I said casually. "Not really sure what to make of it."

"I'll tell you what to make of it," Carson's tone was dead serious. "She's insane. You need to keep your distance from that crazy loon and her made-up religion."

"I think you're overreacting," I said. "I know you don't believe in this stuff...but what if there is a God? Wouldn't you want to know?"

"Nope." Carson's eyes were hard. Clearly, we had reached the end of our conversation.

Monday arrived too early, always the perpetually premature guest that shows up before you're ready. At least I finished school early on Mondays and didn't have to work a night shift at the restaurant, so it was actually a light day for me.

I arrived at school and started getting set up for the day, when I caught a whiff of Ms. Ruth's perfume preceding her arrival around the corner.

"Hey, kid!" she beamed. "Thought of you over the weekend. A few of us are going to have sort of a 'Bible 101' study group in the breakroom after school on Mondays. Just forty-five minutes or so. Wanna come?"

"Hmmm..." I wasn't sure what to say. This certainly wouldn't tally with Carson's warning to steer clear of Ms. Ruth's religious stuff. But I was still curious. "Not sure if that will work with my schedule," I fibbed. "Can I let you know?"

"Take all the time you need," Ms. Ruth smiled. "No pressure, just wanted to extend the invitation."

Pressure or not, her invitation haunted me for weeks. I really wanted to know what it would be like, but Carson had me spooked about being brainwashed. Although, I couldn't really see that happening. Ms. Ruth may be unusual, but Carson had the wrong idea about her.

I knew Debbie was probably one of the girls that was meeting with Ms. Ruth, so I pumped her for information.

"Hey, how's that Bible study going?" I asked. I was trying to seem nonchalant, but for some reason my heart was racing.

"Ooh, it's so good!" she gushed. "Ms. Ruth is such a breath of fresh air. It's like God is right there with us."

"Oh, that's...*nice*." I actually wasn't sure that it sounded nice at all to have God right there with you. Honestly, it sounded potentially terrifying. And weird. And...

Something was stirring inside me. I didn't know what, but I needed to find out what Ms. Ruth and these students had that I didn't. As all of this was spinning in my mind, Ms. Ruth entered the room, as if on cue. Before I could change my mind, I blurted out, "Hey, Ms. Ruth, do you care if I show up for that Bible study?"

"Heck no, kid."

"Does that mean heck no, yes? Or heck no, no?" I asked, half hoping the answer was no.

Ms. Ruth laughed her rich velvety laugh, and shaking her head at me said, "Just stay after school and join us."

"But I don't have a Bible. Was I supposed to read something ahead of time?"

"Don't worry about a thing. All you've gotta do is show up.

We'll have plenty to talk about."

There were about six of us, sitting on folding chairs arranged in a circle. Talk about awkward. If I could have gotten up right then without being rude, I totally would have bolted.

Ms. Ruth seemed to sense my nerves. She looked directly at me and said, "I'm going to open us up with prayer and then we'll get started, okay?" She looked up. "Heavenly Father, thank you for today. Would you reveal your truth? Please show us who you are."

Oh man, feels like I'm back in church—stuck listening to rambling words that mean nothing to me.

Ms. Ruth was still talking, but her voice started to sound like one of the grown-ups on *Charlie Brown*, "Wa-wah, wa-wah, wa, wah." Somehow, I got ahold of myself and tuned back in. Ms. Ruth had finished praying and moved on to asking questions.

"Why do you think God created us? Any thoughts?"

The others took turns answering while I looked for a rock to crawl under. I tried to avoid making eye contact with Ms. Ruth, but she caught me. Thankfully, when her gracious eyes met mine, it wasn't so bad after all.

"What do you think, David?" she asked gently. It seemed like she genuinely wanted to know what I thought. Also, she'd never called me David before. Hearing her speak my name really touched me for some reason.

I thought about it for a bit, but had no idea. My mind was a complete blank. Then I started to wonder if maybe God created us because he was lonely. Maybe he wanted company. I knew a little something about loneliness, about wanting someone to love you back the way you loved them.

Did God and I possibly have something in common?

Another thought interrupted.

Nah, Dummy. He's GOD. Why would he want a gay farm boy as a friend? He's got plenty of angels to keep him company.

I decided not to share my answer with the group. I shrugged instead and vowed not to come back next week.

A few days later, I dragged myself to school bright and early, in spite of a long night at the restaurant the previous evening.

"Morning, kid," Ms. Ruth greeted me in her usual upbeat tone. "Brought you something."

I wasn't fully awake yet and my brain couldn't catch up to the fact that I was being given a present for no reason. Unwrapping it seemed to take forever as I fumbled with the paper, feeling awkward as Debbie and Ms. Ruth watched patiently. I timidly opened the box and saw just what I'd been afraid I might see. I felt a conflicting flood of emotions, ranging from immense gratitude to overwhelming anxiety (fueled by a sense of embarrassment and dread).

"Is this a Bible?" asking the obvious, I was stalling for time to compose my reaction.

"Sure is," Ms. Ruth chuckled. Seemed she always saw right through me.

"Wow…thank you," I finally managed, picking up the book. I held it carefully, as if it were a dangerous snake or a priceless treasure—I wasn't sure which. I thumbed through the first few pages, assuming I'd start at the beginning, as you would with any other book. Ms. Ruth held out her hands, gesturing for me to give the Bible to her. She opened it up about three-quarters of the way through.

"Try starting with the book of John, okay?" She put her hand lightly on my shoulder. "Any questions, just ask."

I nodded and manufactured a smile, then immediately took the thing to my car so no one would see me with it.

Driving to work the next day, I couldn't get that Bible out of my head. It was still under my seat where I'd stashed it and it was kind of creeping me out.

You're being ridiculous, I told myself. *What's the big deal? It's just a book.*

I'd said I wanted to read it someday, so now was as good a time as ever. But Carson would freak if he saw it. And what would my friends say?

I decided to risk it. When I got home that night, I smuggled the book inside and put it in my nightstand drawer.

Carson usually went to bed before me since he had to wake up early. He slept like the dead and rarely stirred when I came in, even if I read before going to sleep. So I wasn't *too* worried about a confrontation.

I went through my usual routine, turning the bedside lamp on and putting a glass of water on the nightstand. After getting settled in bed and making sure Carson was still asleep, I opened the drawer and pulled out the Bible. I stared at it, sizing it up as if this was a showdown, like in the cowboy movies I used to watch as a boy. I opened it about where Ms. Ruth had shown me, and then carefully turned a few of the onionskin pages until I came to John.

The first few words read, "In the beginning...." I paused and took a deep breath.

Here we go…

I didn't fully grasp everything in the opening paragraphs. The style took some getting used to, like watching a movie with subtitles. But soon enough, it started reading like an interesting story. By chapter 3, I was mesmerized. I wasn't sure I could believe what I was reading. It was somewhat familiar, stuff I'd probably heard before (maybe in church on the days I was listening). But somehow reading it for myself made it seem like it was actually written to me.

It said God loved the world so much—*which included me, right?*—that he gave his one and only son, so that everyone who believes in him will have eternal life. Could this be true? I wanted it to be true.

The next day, I couldn't wait to talk to Ms. Ruth.

"I started reading John last night…" I hesitated, not sure what else to say.

"Well, don't leave me in suspense, kid. What'd you think?"

"I liked what it had to say, but I'm not sure it can be true," I admitted. I knew it was important to be honest with her if I was going to sort this out.

"Do me a favor, David," she said, using my name that way of hers that always caught my attention. "When you open the Bible, just ask God to show you the truth, real simple. That's it!"

So that night, I did what Ms. Ruth suggested and was amazed that God actually seemed to answer my prayer. The Bible was unlike any book I'd ever read. The words came alive in my mind and soul in a way I'd never have believed possible if I hadn't experienced it myself. I couldn't get enough of it.

Carson woke up while I was reading. He glanced at me sleepily, did a double take, then rolled over and stared at me.

"*What. Is that?*" he asked, eyeing the book as if it were a potentially diseased stray cat that I'd allowed to curl up on my lap.

"The Bible," I said, matter-of-factly.

"You've *got* to be kidding me," he sighed, rolling his eyes. "You're not starting to buy into that crap, are you?"

"I don't know," I lied, hoping to placate him. "But I want to finish it."

Several weeks went by and I continued my routine: school, work, Bible, sleep, repeat. I felt like I was slowly being drawn into another world and needed to talk to someone who was more neutral about all of this God stuff. I decided to open up to Emma after work one night. She'd asked how school was going, so that seemed like a pretty good segue.

"Really good. I love it—great people." I paused then added nonchalantly, "Oh, and I started reading the Bible."

"What!?" she practically screamed. "Are you kidding? You're just messing with me, right?"

"Nope." I had to laugh at the look of disbelief on her face. "It's true," I said, holding up three fingers to pledge Scout's honor.

"Well, praise the Lord!" she exclaimed, as if I'd won the lottery. I shushed her and smiled sheepishly at a couple of coworkers that were staring at us.

"Sorry," she said, overcompensating by whispering now. "I'm just so excited for you!"

Sheesh. So much for finding someone neutral.

I knew Emma believed in God, but didn't realize she was fanatical like Ms. Ruth. I started to get a little worried that maybe Carson was right. Maybe reading the Bible damaged your brain cells.

I pushed any concerns aside and continued my nightly reading, trying to stay under Carson's radar. Most of what I read was encouraging and helpful, but some of it was really hard to take. The Bible addressed homosexual activity right along with things like murder, adultery, lying, theft, drunkenness—even gossip. No worse. No better. It was all sin.

I wasn't fond of that word, *sin*. Brought me right back to my "Thou shall not" days in Sunday school. Not to mention, according to the things listed as sin, I could check off a few too many for my liking. Guess I shouldn't have been surprised; I'd often felt conflicted about some of my choices and assumed God was unhappy with me. But here I was trying to please him, to do something good by reading the Bible, only to find all of my "sins" staring me in the face. I wondered if this book just might be a snake after all.

Maybe I could just read the Jesus parts, I thought. *I really like that guy, but his dad seems a little harsh.*

That night, I'd drifted off while reading. At some point, I woke up and saw a massive black cloud coming toward me. It engulfed me in the darkest dark and thickest air I'd ever known. The heaviness all around was unbelievable; I could hardly breathe. Then a deep, thunderous voice roared, "You shall worship me!"

I bolted up, and the cloud was gone. Amazingly, Carson was still asleep. *Figures.*

Had I been dreaming? No, I was almost sure I'd been awake. Terrified, I pulled the blankets as high to my chin as they would go and hid my head under the pillow. Several hours passed before I was finally able to fall back asleep.

The next day at school, I grabbed Debbie right away. "Can we go outside?" I asked. "I need to talk to you."

"What's wrong?" she asked, reading my body language with a concerned look.

"I think God spoke to me last night," I said. "Really? Wow! Tell me about it."

So I recounted what had happened. I noticed as I was talking that Debbie became very still. When I'd finished, the color had drained from her face. Whatever she was thinking, it wasn't good.

In her sweet, gentle way, she took me by both arms and looked straight into my eyes.

"Sweetie…" she said slowly, "I don't think that was God."

"What? What do you mean?"

"Honey, God doesn't talk to his children like that."

"Well, if it wasn't God then—"

"I think it might have been Satan," Debbie said solemnly.

I felt sick. It made sense, I guess, but I didn't want to believe it. I suppose I should be relieved that it hadn't been God since whoever it was seemed pretty darn dark and scary. Even so, I was disappointed too. I'd tried to convince myself the visit had been a sign of God's approval and encouragement to keep going. The thought that it might have been Satan was unnerving, to say the least.

I had no way of knowing all of the implications of this event, not only in the physical realm, but in the spiritual realm as well. The battle for my soul was heating up. I knew nothing about the supernatural world. Wasn't that just stuff religious people made up to scare or trick people into believing in God (or giving them money)?

But then, I knew what I saw. It really happened; I had no doubt about that. To say I was confused and freaked out was an understatement of—yes, biblical proportions.

HINDSIGHT REVELATIONS:
WHY READ THE BIBLE?

After decades of reading the Bible, I believe I can confirm it is a priceless treasure—definitely not a snake. Are some parts hard to believe? Can it be difficult to understand? Yes and yes. But it's a special sort of book, one that's best read with your heart as much as your head.

Ms. Ruth's advice to ask God to "show me the truth" before reading has stuck with me to this day. It's easy to mistake, misinterpret (or completely miss) the beauty and intent of the Bible. It's best read *with* God, while keeping an open heart and mind. That's how it becomes alive and personal.

Another common mistake is to assume that what God says to *you* through the Bible is the exact same thing he wants to say to someone else. Not that his core truth is relative or changeable—God is the same yesterday, today, and forever. But he does meet us individually. And there are many nuances of Scripture that were originally written for different people in different contexts. Yet I can read those same texts today and if I'm open to what he wants to say to me, they can be applicable to my unique situation—*and* to my neighbor in an equally unique way. It's pretty crazy.

Some people say the Bible is just a book (or worse), but maybe they haven't read it the right way—yet. If you've never given it a shot, consider yourself invited and encouraged to do so.

For me, deciding to read the Bible was one of the best decisions I ever made. It has made a positive and lasting impact on my life in ways that seemed unimaginable. It took me awhile to (a) believe it was all true, (b) make peace with what it says, then (c) learn how God wants me to apply what I read. Sometimes I can still find any one of these areas a challenge. But I keep pressing on, asking God to show me his truth.

PART TWO

LEARNING TO FLY

Like a fluttering sparrow or a darting swallow, an undeserved curse does not come to rest.

—Proverbs 26:2

Even youths grow tired and weary, and young men stumble and fall; but those who hope in the LORD will renew their strength.

They will soar on wings like eagles; they will run and not grow weary, they will walk and not be faint.

—Isaiah 40:30–31

IN TIME, the mother bird will stand farther away from the nest, motivating her young to venture out onto the branch and take flight. The bird may fall several times, but will eventually learn to ease its falls by spreading its wings. Soon it will attempt to flap its wings more and more.

Although the bird has now experienced flight, this does not make subsequent attempts smooth or easy. The bird may flail its wings clumsily and only sustain flight for a few seconds. Only with practice, will the bird develop the muscles necessary to soar to its full potential.

Meanwhile, the mother bird perches in a safe place and stays watchful overhead. If she senses danger, she may swoop down to intervene as necessary, but more often simply calls her young back to her side.

11

REBIRTH

MID-TWENTIES

I SAT WITH my forehead on the steering wheel of my black Jetta, more than a little buzzed after a late night of drinking. Earlier that night, I'd had yet another strange spiritual experience. It had only been a few days since my encounter with the voice in the dark cloud—now this?

What the hell was happening to me?

Hell. I wondered if tonight's incident was caused by another visitor from hell (wherever or whatever that was). I couldn't shake what Debbie had concluded about my first experience. I knew what I'd seen and felt had been real, so I didn't necessarily feel crazy, but it was still messing with my mind. Was Satan really after me? Did I even believe there was a devil? I realized now that my first visitor probably hadn't been God. Did that mean it was an evil presence?

This thought made me weak in the knees. Then a realization hit me—if it's true that evil spirits exist, that means there must be good spirits too.

So God is real, even if I haven't met him yet.

I wasn't sure in that moment if that was good news for me or not. I'd been living haphazardly, not worrying about any of this stuff. Now it seemed there were two clear choices before me: good or evil.

If Satan had called me to worship him, what did that mean? That he actually thought I was a candidate? I would never do that.

Would I?

Suddenly, there was another voice in my head asking counter-questions.

Where was God when all of this went down? Why hadn't he been the one to visit?

Did he even care?

I waited, not sure what I was waiting for. Nothing happened.

But something *had* happened earlier tonight. What had that been all about?

My mind replayed the events of the evening.

In some ways, it had been a great night. I'd worked the dinner shift at the restaurant. After the last customers were finally ushered out (there's always *that* table, the one that lingers too long), the other waiters and I grabbed a few drinks. It was never so much about the drinking for me, not really. I just loved to laugh with my friends.

But that night, even as the laughter rolled at high tide, something changed. It was as if someone pulled the plug and the ocean of merriment was spiraling down the drain.

We'd been sitting at our usual table, counting tips and nursing drinks, when one of the guys had cried out, *"Jesus Christ!"*

I'm not sure what triggered his outburst. Maybe a spilled drink? All I remembered was the laughter—it swirled around on every side, taunting me as if this was suddenly personal.

I wasn't laughing along this time. I can't explain what came over me, but I wanted to scream at my friend, to make him shut up. It felt like he had called down some kind of spirit. Good, bad…I didn't know. Was my visitor returning? I felt electric and numb all at once. I had to get out of there. Everything else was a blur.

How long had I been sitting in my car now? Hours at least. I stared ahead, wishing there was a picturesque view to help take my mind off things. Instead, I resorted to counting our townhouse staircases and the sets of windows that repeated every fifteen feet or so. I just sat there, feeling like I couldn't move. I was afraid to go inside. Who knows what might be waiting for me there? Another black cloud?

I tried again to clear my head. I'd never seen anyone tending to the landscaping in my everyday comings and goings, but I noticed spring flowers coming up. To my raw state of mind, they seemed magical—inspiring in their struggle to bring beauty to the concrete world around. My mother used to plant those same yellow flowers (daffodils, I think) around the outside of our porch. They looked so fragile right now with their heads bowed, all closed up. They looked like I felt. Sad, almost broken.

Vulnerable. Yet the flowers had something I didn't. They knew what they were supposed to do next. I didn't have a clue.

My mind meandered to the farm. What would the folks be doing today? Probably the same thing they did every day. Actually, they'd be asleep right now. Like most normal people. Like I should be.

I started arguing with myself.

It's two thirty in the morning, David. For God's sake, go to bed.

No. You don't have to go to bed if you don't feel like it. Your whole life, everyone has told you what to do: Go to bed. Clean the barn. Feed the chickens. Make your bed. Cut your hair. Do this. Don't do that. Stop living with Carson—

Just go to bed already.

But I didn't. For some reason, I still felt like I was waiting for something to happen. Probably couldn't fall asleep anyway. I thought about going downtown to hit a couple of the after-hours bars, but Carson was asleep and I didn't want to go by myself. Then I remembered that I had school in just a few hours.

Jesus H. Christ.

"Sorry! I didn't mean it," I said aloud in a panic. I held my breath, worried the thing from the bar would come back.

Great, now I'm talking to Jesus, like Ms. *Ruth. This is stupid…no one is here. I'm talking to the roof of my car.*

A recent conversation with Ms. Ruth came to mind.

"Kid," she'd said in her honey-dipped drawl, "you don't have to fold your hands to talk to Jesus. You don't have to have all the right words in just the right order. God is ready anytime you are. He's waiting for you, you know."

"Waiting for what?" I'd asked.

"Waiting for you to acknowledge him."

"I already believe in God," I'd reminded her. "Church every Sunday as a kid. Communion first Sunday of every month. Confirmed in ninth grade. I'm signed and sealed."

She'd smiled her smile that made you feel like you were being hugged. It was a patient mother's smile as she helps her four-year-old unknot his shoe and tries teaching him to tie it again—rabbit ears, around the tree, through the hole.

"Oh, David, honey, I'm not talking about going through the motions. I want you to meet God in person. Talk to him like you would talk to a friend. Tell him the stuff that no one else knows or cares about."

I ran my hands up and down the leather steering wheel and shifted in my seat while Ms. Ruth's words echoed through the halls of my mind. The wind had picked up a bit outside, sending a chill through me, even though I was incubated by my car. Maybe the wind hadn't caused the chill.

Talk to God? Like a friend? That sounded so weird to me. Wrong even. God wasn't a friend, he was…well, I wasn't exactly sure what (who?) he was. But I knew I was supposed to be reverent—not all, "Hey, dude!" I smiled at the idea of God as a long-haired surfer in board shorts, sporting a sun-blocked nose and holding a giant pizza.

Maybe Jesus, though. I could picture him as a friend. And he had long hair, right? Dude probably fits him better.

I thought about this for a while. Could I really talk to Jesus?

Oh, why not… "So, Jesus…" Long pause.

"I'm thinking I need you to show up now. Okay?"

I felt like an idiot talking out loud, maybe to no one. I waited some more.

Nothing. No answer.

Exactly.

Frustrated, I pulled my keys from the ignition with a huff and hastily grabbed my to-go cup, sloshing the contents over its lip. In a mirrored response, an array of obscenities spilled out of my lips. I started to open the driver's side door and make my escape, but something tugged at me, literally. Spooked, I looked down for a hand or something. I rolled my eyes as I discovered that the hem of my coat was caught on the emergency brake handle.

I was feeling more ridiculous by the minute.

Seriously, Lowry? You're losing it.

Crazy or not, it had been enough to make me reconsider getting out of the car. It felt safer to stay here. I settled back into my seat, took a swig of my drink, and set it back in the cup holder.

Deep breath.

"Okay…" *Just talk to him like a friend*, I reminded myself. "So I have this confession. But if you think I should, like, wait and tell someone else, that's cool…dude."

My sarcastic irreverence amused me for second and I somehow felt that just maybe Jesus was smiling with me. Then my thoughts turned serious again.

Another deep breath.

"So, yeah. You probably already know this, but I don't know what you think about it. I'm…"

I'm what? What am I?

Just say it—you're a faggot, that's what.

Stop it. Shut up! It's not my fault. I didn't make myself this way—

"Okay, yeah. Let's talk about *that*, GOD. Tell me why I'm gay and my brothers—same exact DNA pool—are all straight? What's up with that? First, YOU make me like this…and then you put all that shit in the Bible against me? F***ing unfair, is what it is."

Oh great, David. Nice.

I imagined myself telling Ms. Ruth about this: "I did it. I prayed, just like you said. You'd be so proud of me. Oh, except…I pretty much cussed God out."

You can't even pray right.

And that's when the tears started. Huge, crocodile tears that gave way to heaving, snotty sobs. I remembered feeling this way when I was twelve—too old to cry, but unable to stop. Echoes of my brothers' taunting raced through my head in mock empathy, *"Ohhh, poor baby girl…"*

COMING OUT

But no amount of effort was going to hold anything back at this point. The dam had broken loose and the lake was chasing the river out of its banks. There were no words. Just these catastrophic, guttural sobs. Was that really me making those noises? It sounded so primal. The pain just kept pouring out. I'd driven my car over the broken dam and plunged into the wild river of tears. I was drowning, gasping for breath.

I didn't know I could cry that hard, that long. How many tears are in the human body? Surely, I would run out soon. I felt as though I'd been turned inside out—there couldn't be anything left inside.

Where the hell is a Kleenex when you need one?

I was forced to wipe my nose on my sleeve. Not pretty, but it was effective in shifting my focus.

Why am I crying, anyway? I mean, it's not like I'm really unhappy. My God, look at the good stuff. Wait...am I still talking to God?

God?

"I'm afraid," I whispered.

More tears. But this time, quiet, resigned. Something shifted with this admission. I pulled the lever on the side of the seat and laid back, looking up at the dome light. Then something really bizarre happened. I started having another conversation in my head, but it wasn't with myself. There was a different voice—this one was gentle, yet firm.

What are you afraid of?

I'm afraid of being this person. Afraid of losing track of who I am.

And who is that exactly? Gay? Is that the truth of who you really are?

Well...I love Carson.

Are you sure?

Yes. I think so, at least. I mean, of course I do. I moved here for him, didn't I? He got me out of Dodge. And we're still together...we said forever, right? I want forever.

So then, why are you afraid?

Maybe there are no forevers for guys like me. I don't really like...me. I hate all of this. I just wish I was different.

A slow-rolling tear punctuated this last thought. I blew my nose into my shirt sleeve—no sense in trying to preserve dignity at this point.

Look, God. You can still fix this, right? I don't really understand the surrender thing. Ms. Ruth said I need to say it, you know, like a deal or a pact. So I surrender and then you, what... kind of take over? Change me?

I wasn't sure what to expect. Maybe not an audible voice exactly, but I expected something. Instead, absolutely nothing happened. The air was thick and heavy, but soft and almost liquidy—womb-like.

So I just sat again. For a long time. I should have been freezing, but it felt hot in the car. I remember sitting still like that back home too. Mother said I could sit for an hour sometimes and not move a muscle, just thinking. Sitting and thinking. Like now.

Okay.

I sighed a long sigh.

Okay?

God...Jesus? Whoever. I don't really get what this might mean...but I surrender.

There was a long pause. I could hear the birds waking up.

Do you hear me?

"I surrender. Okay?" I said aloud, maybe a little too defiantly. "Happy?"

I didn't know if I had to say or do anything else, but I wanted to make sure and cover my bases, so I pulled the seat upright and lifted my hands up. They hit the roof of the car.

Well, that was stupid.

I had to laugh. I'd always been able to laugh at myself. Sometimes in moments like this, I imagined that someone was secretly filming me. I could almost hear the audience—that canned sitcom laughter.

Who knows, maybe there *was* an audience. Maybe the angels were smiling. I had no idea about any of that stuff.

All I know is, in that moment, I didn't feel alone.

"So…you can have me. But I could use a little help here, you know? I don't know what I want, but I need to know for sure that you're real."

Silence.

Not knowing what else to do, I got out of the car. I didn't really feel any different. Just tired, completely spent. I imagined how exhausted I'd be at school later—envisioned myself putting someone's hair color in, then falling asleep while it processed. I'd had a nightmare like that once which ended with the woman's hair falling out in my hands. I shuddered at the thought.

It was almost dawn by now. The world yawned and stretched as it eased into morning. I poured what was left of my drink in the grass and lumbered up the stairs to our apartment. I felt much heavier than my 152 pounds, as if a sandbag was tied to each foot.

I unlocked the door and tried to sneak in quietly, but I doubted Carson would wake up, so it didn't really mat—*ouch!* My hand instantly reached down to console the throbbing pain in my shinbone. *Stupid chair.* Carson always forgot to leave a light on for me.

Suddenly forgetting about my pain, I stood very still.

Something didn't feel right. *I* didn't feel right. Not sick, just kind of dizzy maybe? No, not dizzy—I just wanted to kneel. Yeah, I wanted to kneel right then. I *needed* to kneel. So I did.

That's when it started. His name poured out of me. Just his name and no other word, wave after wave.

"Jesus."

And again, "Jesus. Jesus. Jesus."

There was more. I mean, more than the name thing. I'm not sure how to describe the sensation, but it felt like I was being stripped. The carpenter knew there was beauty beneath and was determined to get back to the original creation. Layer by layer, he addressed each stained, painted-on version of my identity, one at a time. And each time, his name, "Jesus," would rise up from deep inside me.

Do it. Just keep on going.

I felt layer after layer peel away, as if my very flesh was being torn—my face, my hands, and finally my heart. It hurt, almost like being burned. But I didn't care. He was taking me down to my core and I knew that was what I needed. Who was I? I had no idea anymore.

"Jesus."

Another layer, not just inside my body, but deeper. My soul was an artichoke—petal by thorn-tipped petal was discarded to get to my heart.

"Jesus."

I was sobbing again, I think. Crying, screaming, laughing. "Jesus."

Ms. Ruth had certainly not prepared me for *this*. I made a mental note to have some serious words with her.

"Jesus."

He wasn't done. Not yet.

And so the remaining hours of the morning were spent, while Carson somehow slept through every minute. He had no idea.

At some point, I didn't feel the urge to say Jesus's name any more. But it was my own name that I heard. And it sounded even sweeter than when Ms. Ruth said it...

David.

And with that, I knew I wouldn't be the same person I'd been the day before. I imagined this was what it felt like to be squeezed through the birth canal, only as an adult. The world you'd once known was gone forever. There was light. There was confusion. Everything was new.

I didn't know who I would be now—like no one I'd ever been before, I supposed. At least, no one I remembered being.

I would be me.

HINDSIGHT REVELATIONS:
TRUE IDENTITY

Not everyone's conversion experience is quite this dramatic, but others are perhaps even more dramatic. As I've said elsewhere, God meets us uniquely, as individuals.

Reflecting on my own experience, I notice how important names and identities are to God. He definitely impressed this upon me in the way Jesus's name became so sacred. Before my first encounter with Jesus, I'd always thought of my identity in terms of how I'd describe myself, something like "David the tall, blond, gay, waiter/student."

The problem with basing our identity on these things is that they're mostly external and potentially subject to change. These descriptions have little to do with who we *really* are at our core, spirit level. The Bible says that in the physical realm, God created us "male and female," but it later goes on to say that in the spiritual realm, there is "neither man nor woman" (this also implies there is neither gay nor straight, since these distinctions are gender-based). So in the physical world, we were created with specific genders according to God's design—but this does not affect our true identity.

We don't have to wait for heaven to embrace this truth.

If you're thinking Ms. Ruth's perfume went to my head, hang with me. Let's go back the physical realm. To a certain degree, I still think of myself as a tall, blond hairstylist. But other things have changed. I'm not a waiter or a student anymore. Nor do I define myself as gay. These things are all descriptive, but they have nothing to do with my true identity.

It pains me to hear people identify themselves as addicts, long after breaking an addiction. Is it good to be on guard against relapsing in areas where we may struggle? Yes. But should a slave be tethered to a ball-and-chain once set free? No—I believe we need to see ourselves as God sees us.

In my spirit, only one identifier matters: I am a child of God. And this is only possible through my identification with Jesus, the firstborn child of God. (This, by the way, is the mystery of the ages—a matter of faith, not reason. So don't worry if you can't wrap your brain around it.)

My name, David, means "beloved," which is highly significant because unconditional love was all I ever wanted. And now I have it. I see myself as a beloved child of the creator of the universe. This is a game changer. It reframes every choice I make and everything that happens to me, whether good or bad. And it's a truth that not even death can change. When I leave this earth, I may no longer be a hairstylist (then again, who knows?). But I do know that I will still be a beloved child of God.

And that mind-blowing, life-altering identity is available to anyone who chooses it.

12

MY COMING-OUT PARTY

MID-TWENTIES

THE NEW ME walked into beauty school that morning feeling pretty much like the old me with an emotional hangover. I needed to talk with Ms. Ruth, ASAP. She wasn't in yet, so I tried starting my lessons but couldn't seem to concentrate. The previous night's events kept playing over and over in my head.

What was that feeling, that sensation I'd felt—the layers peeling off like Saran Wrap every time I said Jesus's name? What did it all mean? I had no clue, but knew I needed to talk to someone that might know what the heck was going on.

"Does anybody know when Ms. Ruth is coming in?" I asked.

A fellow student said she was supposed to be in at noon. It was going to be a long morning.

Finally, lunchtime came. I lit up a smoke and took a big puff, nervous about what I was going to tell Ms. Ruth. But when she opened the door, I felt a wave of comfort wash over me. It was all I could do to stop myself from falling into her arms like I had with my mother as a child.

"Hiya, kid, how's your day going?"

"You won't believe this, Ms. Ruth. Something happened last night..." I proceeded to share every emotional detail.

She came close to me, almost nose to nose, with an intense look on her face. She always had a special way about her, but I'd never seen this expression—she had tears in her eyes. I worried that something was wrong, that she was going to tell me I was crazy. But then she smiled one of the biggest smiles I've ever seen and grabbed my chin as she pulled me in and kissed my forehead, probably leaving a giant red lipstick mark.

"David, that was Jesus ripping those layers right off! I've never experienced anything quite like that, but he has his way of getting to the heart of the matter with each of us. Last night...you gave your life to Christ."

Our hug seemed to last for hours. I didn't want it to end. It was as though her acknowledgment of what had happened gave me permission to feel everything I'd been hoping for, but I was afraid it was too good to be true. The sense of acceptance was overwhelming. The shame and guilt I'd been carrying for years was lifted off. I'm surprised I didn't float right up to the ceiling when she finally let go of me.

"So what do I do now?"

"Well, you just keep reading that Bible and talking to God."

"He'll show you."

She gave me another big squeeze, then left me to my thoughts.

Did she say God? Wait a minute, I had an encounter with Jesus.

It was Jesus who had shown up.

At this point, Jesus and God were very separate entities in my mind. I was pretty confused about the way all of this worked. I figured Jesus talked to his dad, so God the Father probably knew what was going on. But I still thought the Big Guy was disappointed with me so it was easier to focus on Jesus instead.

I quickly pushed these worries and questions away, not wanting to let anything interfere with how good I'd felt moments ago.

At least I've got Jesus on my side now; Ms. Ruth said so. And he's all I need to get to heaven, right?

I was pretty sure that's what I'd read. I could figure out the God thing later.

I went straight from school to my restaurant shift, exhausted but carried by a sense of exhilaration. It was like a nonstop adrenaline rush—better than any drug I'd ever tried, none of which had really appealed to me (the last thing *I* needed was to feel paranoid or out of control). This spiritual buzz, on the other hand, left me feeling wonderful in every way.

I couldn't wait to tell Emma and caught her just as she was taking an order out to customers.

"I asked Jesus into my heart last night," I whispered as she walked by.

Emma stopped dead in her tracks, then did a U-turn, setting the tray of drinks she'd been balancing down on the bar. She wrapped her arms around me with such enthusiasm that somebody told us to get a room.

"I've been praying for this since the day I met you!" she confided.

It was strange to realize how many people had been praying or gently nudging me toward Jesus. I'd had no idea.

I drove home that night feeling pretty much like the same ol' David now that my spiritual high had ebbed. My desperate need for sleep was taking over my brain. But I *had* noticed one thing. After close, one of my coworkers had too much to drink.

Usually, I would have just ignored this and let him go about his way, but something prompted me to take care of him and make sure he got home safely.

I still smoked and drank and cussed just like before, so it wasn't like I'd been consciously trying to be hyper-spiritual. But I went out of my way to help someone even though it was inconvenient. That would have been completely out of character for me yesterday. I was interested to see what else might be different now.

But as the days went by, disappointment started to set in. I had assumed that the work Jesus had done in dissecting and rebuilding my soul would bring lasting relief. I'd expected my rebirth to throw the doors wide open to a new life filled with wonder and joy and endless spiritual insights.

Instead, everything looked pretty much the same as it always had: another day at school, another evening serving tables, another night at the bars—and of course, Carson was still in my bed. I believed that I was different inside, but I didn't really *feel* that different anymore. The rush had worn off, and it seemed like my life was back to the usual humdrum. Guess the honeymoon was over.

I needed to know more. I read my Bible, asked questions, prayed, called out to Jesus for understanding, and surrendered daily. I hoped maybe he'd visit again, maybe under less intense circumstances. I also cried—a lot. I'd always been sensitive, but now *everything* seemed to make me cry. I sure hoped Jesus had something better than this in store.

One day, I cornered Debbie at school, hoping for some answers. "What now? What do I do next?"

"Maybe you should get baptized," she suggested.

"I already did that—well, my parents did anyway, when I was a baby."

"That was probably more of a dedication," she said. "Different people believe different things about baptism. I see something beautifully symbolic about being totally immersed in water—like burying your old life and rising to a new one. Jesus was baptized, you know. You might think of it as a public confession that you've decided to follow him. Like a wedding ceremony."

Public? I wasn't sure I wanted the world to know—especially Carson and my friends.

"Hmmm, let me think about it," I said. "I'll let you know."

My nightly Bible reading really started to affect my relationship with Carson. He would often look at me in disgust. I wasn't too sure about my feeling for him either. I felt us growing further and further apart. I knew I needed to tell him what had happened last week and see how he felt about my baptism.

There wasn't really good a way to ease into the conversation. ("Hey, I really like that shirt. The colors remind me of Christmas. Speaking of Christmas, I met Jesus the other night. Did I mention I like your shirt?")

I decided to just come out with it. "I asked Jesus into my life," I said.

Carson rolled his eyes. It was becoming his standard response to me.

"What does that mean, exactly?" he asked. "You gonna run off and become one of those holy rollers on TV? *'O help us, Jee-sus!'*" He raised shaking hands in mock surrender and attempted his best Southern Baptist preacher accent. Carson always had a flare for the dramatic.

"No," I said, trying not to get annoyed. "It means I believe he's the Son of God. He paid the price for my sins and he's coming back—"

"Woah, that's a lot of sins. You sure about that?" Carson was getting wound up. I could see his sarcastic wheels turning and knew I was in for it.

"What do you mean 'coming back'? Where's he been... Bloomingdales?"

"He's coming back on a white horse, out of heaven." I winced as I said it, knowing how ridiculous it sounded. But I believed every word.

I waited for Carson's next hilarious quip. But it never came.

Instead, he got angry. Really angry. He slammed the last of his drink, bringing the glass down on the table so hard I was afraid it might shatter. Then he stared at me, his dark eyes narrowing into black slits.

"Look," he said. "I don't know what kind of cult Kool-Aid you've been drinking, but I'm not listening to any more of this horseshit."

He nearly knocked the table over as he got up. A few seconds later, I heard the bedroom door slam.

I knew I was going to have to do this without Carson.

It was looking like I would be doing a lot of things without him.

The next few weeks at home were chilly to say the least. Carson and I mostly tried to avoid each other, which wasn't too hard, given my schedule. I decided to sleep on the couch.

Meanwhile, Debbie wouldn't seem to let the baptism thing go.

She kept saying how important it was. "What's the big deal? I'm saved, right?"

"Yes, of course," she said. "But there's so much more beyond being saved. Imagine you're given a free ticket to a concert. You wouldn't wait in line to pay for a ticket you already have. The concert has already started—if you want to hear the music, you have to go inside. And the closer you get to the stage, the better it's going to sound. Getting baptized is like moving closer, pressing in."

I kinda-sorta got what she was saying, but wasn't really sure. She tried again.

"Baptism is symbolic of washing sins away. It's a way of repenting."

Ugh. This was starting to seem like church again. Debbie noticed that I recoiled a little.

"I know some people have a problem with the word repent since there's a lot of religious history wrapped around it. But it really just means you've changed your mind about the way you want to live. It's a way to show obedience to God."

"Yeah, well…" I said with a little more attitude than intended, "the Bible says a lot of things about obedience. I don't think I'm quite there yet, okay?"

I suddenly felt anxious for some reason. Hadn't I already surrendered? When would it be enough? But on the other hand, I guess it couldn't hurt anything. Carson was already ticked. I'd known for a while now that I was going to have to make some hard choices.

I'll do it in a couple of weeks, I decided.

Apparently, Ms. Ruth and Debbie had other thoughts about that. That afternoon, Ms. Ruth told me she'd talked to the pastor at Debbie's church. He could baptize me right after school, that very day if I wanted. I was puzzled by the rush, but they weren't pushy—just said the opportunity was available. Maybe they knew something I didn't. Maybe this would help me get over the hump and really commit myself. I trusted them and the more I thought about it, the more I wanted to do it.

What the heck, so I'll go get a little wet.

I showed up at the church and met with the pastor. He seemed nice enough—not the foreboding figure I remembered my childhood minister to be. The pastor smiled at me as he stepped into the baptismal tank. His presence stirred the water as he moved closer to take his place next to me. I shivered a little. Not sure if this was due to nerves or the cool water moving around me. I looked for reassurance from Ms. Ruth and Debbie, who were standing by me outside of the tank. Ms. Ruth gave me her signature wink and I relaxed a bit.

The pastor asked if I'd accepted Jesus into my life.

I answered, "Yes," and could feel the importance of the word as I said it.

Then he said, "David, I baptize you in the name of the Father, Son, and Holy Spirit."

I held my breath and went under the water. When I came up, it was as if the place was one hundred watts brighter. I heard applause and felt overwhelmed by love. About forty people had come to witness my baptism and I'd only decided to go through with it a few hours ago. Guess good news travels fast in God's kingdom.

Ms. Ruth beamed at me.

"The angels in heaven are rejoicing too. Welcome to the family, kid!"

HINDSIGHT REVELATIONS:
WHY BAPTISM?

I hadn't thought about it this way at the time, but baptism is a kind of coming out. It's stepping from one life into another. It's a declaration to the world, confessing the truth of who you really are. Announcing that you're putting Jesus first in your life.

It doesn't matter how you might have perceived your identity before (gay, straight, bi, addict, alcoholic, republican, democrat—whatever). Baptism represents burying that old identity and coming out of that life, into a completely new core identity. It's the marker of a journey to begin realizing and becoming the best version of yourself.

I still didn't really understand my sexuality at this time, so it's important to note that baptism isn't a magical elixir that erases every desire. Profound things can happen in the spiritual world, which take time to work out in the physical world.

The transformation of a caterpillar to a butterfly offers an amazing illustration. When the caterpillar molts into a chrysalis, he dies to his old life. When he emerges, he is a new creature. But he can't fly right away. It takes time for him to stretch his wings. Even though he's a butterfly now, he has to wait for his body to catch up to that reality.

In human terms, it may take most of our earthly lives to complete this transformation process, to fully realize who we really are, to stretch our wings and fly. But that doesn't change the fact that our identity as a new creation is complete when we receive the life Jesus offers.

13

EXODUS

MID-TWENTIES

FOLLOWING my baptism, as the weeks turned into months my "Jesus high" seemed to ebb and flow. I found it frustrating that my new beliefs weren't easily lining up with my everyday experiences. I was still living with Carson and wasn't quite sure what to do about that situation. It felt like my life had already been turned upside down. I didn't know if I could take much more change at this point.

All I had to hold on to was my Bible, Ms. Ruth, and a few televangelists who were always asking me to put my hands on the TV screen for healing. Although some of them may not have been all they claimed to be, these preachers became my life thread. Their supernatural world was new and exciting to me. Their promises of redemption, transformation, and healing offered me hope. Better still, doing church through the television offered a judgment-free zone. I pressed on in faith, determined to find the truth.

My weekly routine looked pretty much the same as it had before, except I was spending less time with Carson and the boys, and more time with Ms. Ruth. We would often use our midday break to grab lunch at our favorite Chinese restaurant. I loved the buffet because it worked well for my shoestring budget—one meal would get me through most the day. Between return trips for sesame chicken, we'd chat about life and, of course, Jesus.

During one of our visits, Ms. Ruth seemed to intuitively notice that I was struggling.

"So, kid, what's the word? You seem a little down."

She was never shy about getting to the heart of the matter. "Honestly? I'm not doing so great these days," I confided. "Isn't being a Christian supposed to make everything better? Make *me* better? Even after being baptized, I'm still messing up all the time. If Jesus was here at our table, what would he say? Do you think he's mad at me?"

"Ah, sweet child," she smiled empathetically, "you might as well know now that following Jesus isn't always easy. And no, I'd bet money he's not mad at you. But why don't you ask him yourself? He's here, all right. His Holy Spirit is always with us."

"You mean the thing my grandma always called the Holy Ghost? I never got that. Aren't ghosts like evil spirits or something?" I'd never really believed in ghosts, but in light of recent experiences, I wasn't ruling much out these days.

"Oh, kid. I'm not talking about Casper—bet your grandma wasn't either," she smiled in her reassuring way that told me my questions were always welcome. And the Holy Spirit is far from evil—he's holy, after all. Says so right in his name. The Spirit of Truth has been with the Father and Jesus since the very beginning. He's known as the helper. Jesus promised to send him to us after his resurrection."

"I guess now that you mention it, I do remember reading about that. But I didn't really get it," I admitted. "So the Holy Spirit is a whole other person…God…uh, thing? Will I meet him too?"

"You already have. God the Father, God the Son, and God the Spirit are always together—and always with you."

"Okay, now I'm really confused," I said with a sigh.

I was just getting to know Jesus, and in a holding pattern with God. Now there was someone else to worry about? Exactly who was I supposed to pray to?

"It is a mystery, that's for sure. To tell you the truth," she lowered her voice in mock secrecy, "I don't know exactly how it all works. I just know it's all good."

Ms. Ruth thought a minute before proceeding.

"If it helps, you might picture a spring bubbling forth from a rock: the Father is the source, Jesus is the way or path, and the Spirit is the water. Jesus called the Spirit 'living water.' When the Holy Spirit flows through us, he offers guidance. He's a teacher and a comforter. He convicts the world of sin…"

I think she kept talking, but I tuned out. I was stuck on the words *convict* and *sin*. I thought of Carson.

"Wait," I said. "So what do you mean 'he convicts'? Like sends people who sin to hell?" *Some comforter.* I kept this comment to myself.

"Hmmm, I think we're getting ahead of ourselves. Maybe a better word than *convicts* is *exposes*. Suppose someone feels sick, but doesn't know why. He goes to the doctor and gets an X-ray that exposes a disease. The good news is, it's totally treatable. But left unchecked, the disease might continue to fester and spread. So in this case, exposure is a good thing. Like bringing something into the light. Does that help?"

I nodded, but wasn't so sure. Ms. Ruth noticed.

"I think that might be enough for today. But listen, it's important for you to know that anything the Holy Spirit shows you is wrapped with love. He always has your best interests in mind. If you ever feel condemned or worthless, that's *not* coming from him. Okay?"

I nodded again, still trying to take it all in.

"Oh, kid!" She slapped the table as we stood up to leave. "I almost forgot one of the best parts. Did I mention that the Holy Spirit is quite the gift giver? Sometime soon, imagine yourself with your hands open to receive and let's just see what happens." As we left, I was stuffed with more than egg rolls and dumplings. The Holy Spirit business put my brain on overload. It felt safer to just focus on Jesus for now. At the same time, I was intrigued.

I found myself replaying our lunch conversation throughout the afternoon. By now, I was an expert at pin curls so putting them in on autopilot gave me time to think. Try as I might, I couldn't quite grasp the concept of the Holy Spirit. But just when I was about to give up, I looked down at my perfect pin curl and had an epiphany. I realized this wasn't so much something I could figure out, not like a math problem. It was more like putting in pin curls. I couldn't get it at first, but it got easier. Maybe if I relaxed into this whole spirit thing and went with the flow, it would just sorta happen. I wondered if the Holy Spirit himself wasn't showing me this.

As I drove home that afternoon, something was different. I suddenly felt full of joy, for no apparent reason. It made no sense—my life was a mess in a lot of ways. But in that moment, I felt content. Peaceful. I looked up at the sky and it was the brightest blue I'd ever seen. Everything I saw seemed like a gift and I was overcome by powerful, wonderful emotion.

"Thank you," I whispered.

When I got home, I had some time to kill until my restaurant shift at five. But it turned out that the Holy Spirit wasn't quite done with me yet. In fact, he was about to introduce himself in a profound way.

I was still feeling peaceful after my experience in the car and decided to relax in the swivel chair. This was usually Carson's spot, but he wasn't home yet so I got both the chair *and* control of the TV. I flipped to *The 700 Club* on the Christian station, hoping to hear about a miracle or something to keep my good spiritual vibes flowing.

A few minutes later, I started feeling tingly all over while this bright cylinder of light came down over me, like a massive flashlight. It felt like something straight out of *Star Trek*—so much so that I worried for a second that I was being beamed up. Then I started hearing music, like a choir. It was the loveliest sound I'd ever heard; exactly what you would imagine angels sounding like. I started singing along, but not in English. It was some sort of heavenly language. The light was so...I guess *pure* is the best way to put it. No words can adequately describe the beauty of the entire experience.

I could stay here forever, I thought.

And then, in a blink, everything was back to normal. I was sitting in my chair just as before. The only light left in the room was my glowing television screen.

What...just happened?

I literally pinched myself.

Nope, wide awake. So what was this? An out-of-body experience? Before I had time to process it any further, the door opened. "Hey, how was your day?" Carson asked nonchalantly, throwing his keys on the coffee table. He did a double take when he actually looked at me. "What's wrong with *you?*"

"What? Oh...nothing," I said, not convincingly. I tried again in a lower octave. "Nothing. Nothing is wrong."

Carson looked at the TV that was still tuned to *The 700 Club*. He shook his head in disgust and walked into the bedroom without another word.

For weeks, I didn't tell a soul about my experience that afternoon. Who would believe such a thing? I felt like Alice in Wonderland: things were getting "curiouser and curiouser." If I started seeing a white rabbit, I was checking myself in. Ironically, drugs had never really been my thing, but here I was having all kinds of trippy experiences.

After this strange encounter, I kept having the recurring thought that I needed to end things with Carson. But I was scared and had no idea how to go about it. Ms. Ruth had said the Holy Spirit was "the helper," so I tried sending up a prayer.

If this is what I'm supposed to do, Holy Spirit, please help me.

The atmosphere grew increasingly tense at home. I'd told a few of our friends about asking Jesus into my life and their reactions weren't exactly warm and fuzzy. I sensed that Carson had reached his threshold. He came home one night in an especially sour mood.

"We need to talk," he said.

That statement never ends well, I thought. *Here we go....*

"Okay, what about?" I asked, even though I already knew the answer.

"You know, this Jesus thing…it isn't what I'm wanting in a relationship."

Long pause.

"So what are you saying, Carson?"

"I'm saying, I think it's time we split up."

"I think so too," I heard myself say.

Immediately after the words were out, fear set in.

What in the world? Did I just agree to this? I've spent the last six years of my life with Carson. What am I going to do now?

There was an awkward silence and an even more awkward hug. And then he left.

It wasn't until later that evening that I wondered if the Holy Spirit actually *had* helped me. I certainly hadn't been expecting Carson to initiate the breakup conversation, but I guess it got the job done. I was sad—nothing about this was easy—but I knew it was the right thing to do. Having peace about that provided some comfort.

The weekend was filled with tears as the news traveled around our inner circle of friends. Some seemed surprised but others weren't. (Carson had probably been complaining about me for a while now.) Regardless of what anyone thought, my decision had been made. It was time to get out of my old surroundings and start walking in the direction I felt the Holy Spirit was leading me.

My new apartment was small (realtors would call it "cozy"). I only wound up with a few pieces of furniture after everything was divvied between us. I didn't get the swivel chair, of course. Too many memories anyway—I needed a fresh start. Even so, I missed the comfort of the familiar. Breaking old habits is never easy. Not to mention, I wasn't just losing Carson; this was much more than a breakup. I knew if I was going to follow Jesus, it meant changing my way of life.

And so, my exit out of the gay lifestyle was not what I would call a happy ending. Some might call it a victory, but I sure didn't feel like celebrating. Now that I'd "come out" as a follower Jesus, many of my old friends didn't want anything to do with me. I hadn't foreseen this rejection. One by one, friendships seemed to fall away.

I was now on the receiving end of the sort of catty remarks I'd once found funny:

"Hey, I hear you're one of those born-again Christians. Do you *really* think you're going to change? You can't simply take gay off like it's a dirty shirt. You'll be back."

This sort of backlash from people I'd thought were my friends almost hurt worse than the breakup.

Old insecurities chimed in with the sad choruses playing in my head. I'd had many of these same feelings when Jill and I broke up. The familiar pain of loneliness and rejection resurfaced.

Was this what my new path had led to? Alone, far from home, to rip open old wounds? And where the heck was Jesus in all of this?

I felt like this was kind of his fault.

I do what he says and everything falls apart. Then he leaves me alone to pick up the pieces? Nice.

That other voice was back.

Maybe you should just go out and find a new boyfriend, it suggested. In that moment, it seemed like a pretty good idea. Maybe this had been a huge mistake. I just wanted everything to feel okay again. I was like the Israelite slaves I'd read about who had been rescued by a big show of God's power when Moses parted the Red Sea. When freedom didn't measure up to their expectations, they began to idealize life in back in Egypt. It seemed easier to be a slave to the cruel master of sin and all I'd known before, than to be free yet feel so unsure.

Then I remembered Ms. Ruth telling me that I'm never alone.

So Jesus must be here, even if it doesn't feel like it.

The tiny seed of faith I had was enough—in the end, it won out over my emotions. My drive to follow Jesus was strong. I was compelled to stay the course.

After a deep breath or two, I didn't feel quite so lonely. Jesus *was* there. So I did have at least one friend left—maybe two if I counted the Holy Spirit as a person. Two friends sounded better than one, so I decided to go with that.

I reminded myself that I still had Ms. Ruth and Debbie...Emma too. Maybe that was the answer. I just needed more friends that loved Jesus. Maybe it was time to look for a church.

HINDSIGHT REVELATIONS:
A WILLING HEART

Individual spiritual experiences are unique and I realize some of the extraordinary things that happened to me may sound hard to believe.

Talking about the Holy Spirit seems to make some people uncomfortable. Perhaps because it's difficult to wrap our minds around him.* Or maybe because it sounds weird or scary to not be in full control of a situation or experience. Some go so far as to say that it's all made up. However, the Bible is full of firsthand accounts describing encounters with the Holy Spirit.

I understand why people might be skeptical of charlatans and exaggerated or fabricated mystical experiences. Unfortunately, this happens. But we can use discernment and wisdom to identify truth from lies. This is all part of having faith. Believing what we can't see. Believing what may not make sense. Or at least being *willing* to believe. In my experience, it started by simply softening my heart to the possibility that the things I was reading and hearing could actually be true.

A willing heart may be the distinguishing factor between those who believe and those who don't yet believe. You might remember back in the very first chapter when I described how working long days in the sun had lightened my hair but

---

* Spirit is neither male nor female, but since we lack a genderless pronoun in respect to personhood I'll use 'he' as the Bible does.

darkened my skin? Exposure to the very same light resulted in opposite reactions: one got lighter, one got darker.

What if God is like that sunlight? What if the condition of our hearts determines our reactions? Unwilling hearts find it difficult to receive truth and choose to stay in the dark because it's all they've known. On the other hand, willing hearts experience an opposite reaction. They're able receive truth, the Light of the World. And the truth sets us free.

14

THE DESERT

MID- TO LATE-TWENTIES

THE SOLITUDE of my apartment was both a blessing and a curse as my post-Carson life continued to unfold. I was finally free to read the Bible in peace and watch whatever I wanted on TV, but I was terribly lonely. My Christian experience was far from any sort of Promised Land I could imagine. It felt much more like no-man's-land—a dry, desolate desert.

Having graduated from beauty school a few months ago, I didn't get to see Ms. Ruth and Debbie as much. I'd taken the first job I could get, at the hospital salon. Doing roller sets for the elderly and trims for sick people was not where I'd expected my career to be heading. But I made the best of it.

When I wasn't at work, I was mostly a wreck. I didn't know what to do with myself, so I'd wind up wandering back to the bars. I usually sat alone—nursing drinks as a spectator, feeling stuck between two different worlds and welcome in neither one. Saturday mornings were brutal. I was usually hung over and hugging the toilet. The last thing I wanted to do was stand behind a salon chair making chitchat all day. But what choice did I have?

As seemed to be his way, God kept putting people in my path to check up on me and nudge me along. One particularly rough morning, a sweet lady with box-dyed burgundy hair (bless her heart) came in for a roller set. She asked how I was doing and it was all I could do to keep it together. I took a deep breath and told her it was tough juggling two jobs. (I was still working at the restaurant too, trying to make ends meet.) I never shared specifically what I was going through. How could I? She said to keep my eyes on Jesus and he'd take care of the rest. I nodded and smiled politely.

But as I stepped outside for a smoke break, I wasn't sure if I believed that was true anymore. A battle was raging inside me. I was like David from the Bible, facing this huge Goliath of a problem. Only I didn't have the confidence that I could win. I knew I needed to change my lifestyle for good. But how? It was what I knew—what felt real to me. I'd tried to make this huge sacrifice for Jesus and right now it seemed like all I'd gotten was loneliness in return. I felt weak and I didn't know how much longer I could hold out.

"I need help," I said aloud, not sure if I was praying or just talking to the wind.

That very evening, I got a call from a well-known hairdresser. He'd seen a guy walking down the street and admired his haircut, so he stopped and asked who did it for him. Turned out, the cut was one of mine (I did "kitchen cuts" after hours at the restaurant for extra cash). The hairdresser offered me a job at his new salon. I had to think about it for precisely zero seconds. Surely, this was an answer to prayer.

This is exactly what I need, I thought. *A boost in my career will take my mind off everything else.*

However, thirty minutes into my first day, I wasn't so sure this new job was the answer I'd hoped it would be. For one thing, I wasn't welcomed as hot new talent. Instead, I was the new kid on the block. Being treated like a clueless rookie didn't help my fragile morale. Worse still, I could tell the salon's party and lifestyle culture was going to present a huge challenge for me. How was I ever going to stay true to Jesus and still fit in here?

But I wasn't going back. I couldn't. All I knew to do was keep praying.

"Jesus, would you come into my life and forgive me of my sins and change me?"

I would often repeat these same words multiple times a day. I know now I only had to do it once. Jesus heard me the first time—he doesn't come in and out of our lives on a whim, or based on our behavior. Even so, saying the words strengthened my resolve.

I didn't hide my faith at work; this was who I was now and I was tired of hiding. It didn't take long for word to get around. Whispers would float into earshot, intertwined with incredulous giggles and comments dripping with sarcasm.

"You know he's gay, right? But he thinks he's a *sinner* and has to change. Isn't that *precious?*"

I eventually made a couple of friends. John and Marcy seemed to like me, so I invited them over one night to get to know them better.

"So...you're a Jesus fan, eh?" Marcy said. "I'm Christian too, so we're the same, right?"

"I assume so," I said, feeling relieved to have something in common with people for a change.

As we sat in my living room, I shared some of my story. I told them about asking Jesus into my life and then splitting up with Carson.

"What does your church say about all this?" Marcy asked. "I don't really have a church yet. Just TV church."

I'd been meaning to look into the whole church thing for a while, but couldn't seem to go through with it. Besides, I was good with TV church for now.

"Uh, you don't believe all that televangelist stuff, do you?" John said. "They just want your money."

"Well, they'll have to get in line," I laughed. "Anyway, I've got my Bible too. I believe it's the truth, like a recipe for my life. I'm just not sure how to mix everything together yet."

"What do you mean?" Marcy asked.

"I know I'm supposed to change, but I don't know how. The Bible says practicing homosexuality is sinful."

John and Marcy exchanged a glance.

"David, there are a lot of people who would disagree with you on that," Marcy said gently. "I'm not even sure the church would agree. There are gay priests and pastors, you know."

"Thanks, Marcy. I know you're trying to help," I said. "But I believe what the Bible says. I have to do things differently now."

"Well, good luck with that," Marcy said. Her tone wasn't quite as kind now. "I'm sorry, but I think you've got this wrong, David. I don't believe you can change something like being gay. It's who you are."

This was a knife to my gut. I wasn't sure how to respond. Here was someone I respected, someone of faith who believed in the same Jesus and read the same the Bible. I suppose what she said would have seemed like good news if I didn't *want* to change, but I felt a tug in my spirit that disagreed with her conclusions.

In the Bible and in nature, I found evidence in God's design—he created us male and female, then told us to be fruitful and multiply. I could also see how Satan uses sexuality as one of his premier devices to confuse and derail us. And I saw that we are called "new creations" when we follow Jesus. Didn't that mean I could change?

How could Marcy and I see things so differently? And how was I supposed to stay strong when people kept challenging me? I considered discussing this further with my new friends, but I didn't know them well enough to feel like it would be a productive conversation at this point. So I tried changing the subject instead. Our interaction still felt uncomfortable and they winded up leaving somewhat abruptly. Unfortunately, they didn't take the gloom that had settled over the room with them.

I walked to the bedroom and stared dejectedly at the mirror.

Who are you kidding? They're right—you haven't changed one bit.

This is hopeless.

Even though I'd broken up with Carson, I was still attracted to men. What if Marcy was right? Maybe I couldn't change. Was I even supposed to? Marcy was a believer and she said gay was okay. There were even gay priests. Had I misunderstood the Bible? But then, what about the televangelists that preached hellfire and brimstone, saying that homosexuals are going straight to hell? This always brought shouts of "Amen!" and thunderous applause from the audience.

Who was right? My life felt like a sham. I'd lost friendships with people who'd said it was important to accept people, no matter what. Apparently, what they meant was, they were all for accepting people—as long as you agreed with *their* worldview. I accepted my friends regardless of their choices. I wasn't telling anyone what to do. I was just trying to find my way.

Was all of this worth it? Was it even real? My supernatural experience with Jesus was beginning to seem like a distant dream. Sure wasn't feeling Jesus's love right now—or any love for that matter.

I tapped into to a conversation that Mom and I had recently that had filled me with hope. I'd asked her about her faith, asked how she knew it was real. Mom told me this story about her father, who had passed away before I was born:

"When your grandfather was dying in the hospital, there was a shortage of nurses. So I helped take care of him. At one point, I became so exhausted that I cried out to God for help. That evening, a nurse with the most beautiful red hair I had ever seen, came in and said she was there to relieve me. She told me it was okay to let go and sent me home to get some rest. I felt a deep sense of peace wash over me.

That night, your grandfather died. When I went in the next morning, I asked for the nurse's name so I could thank her for taking care of Dad in his final hours. They looked at me in dismay, saying there weren't any nurses with red hair working at this hospital. But I know what I saw. I know it was God's answer to my prayer.

So yes, Son, it's real—angels, heaven, God, Jesus—all of it. It's real."

Remembering this helped, but Mom wasn't here right now to reassure me. No one was. My spiritual walk was wobbly and unsteady. I was a one-year-old tiptoeing precariously forward without a hand to hold. Falling seemed like the only thing I was good at. I wound up face-to-the-floor, sobbing, willing my life to change. I felt so deeply alone. The only company I had were guilt, shame, and a constant sense of failure. I was ready to call it quits.

I was choking on a heavy darkness that never seemed to lift, as if I were in a deep dungeon that sunlight couldn't reach. Maybe the only way out of this entire mess was to end my life. Would anyone even care? Maybe my family, but they were far away and could never understand what I was going through. Emma had moved to Atlanta. Ms. Ruth and

Debbie were probably tired of my constant questions and lack of progress by now (this wasn't true, but that was my thinking). My TV church wouldn't miss me. They wouldn't even know I'd left.

Then a name came into my mind. It was a crazy thought, so I dismissed it immediately.

But the thought came again.

Write Pat Robertson.

The TV preacher? Could this man of God really care about some guy in Indianapolis? Doubtful, but I'd always thought something was different about his demeanor. When he talked, it felt almost like he was speaking to me personally. What did I have to lose? It was the reach of the century, but I decided if he believed all he said and truly cared about me, I was going to find out.

Desperate for any lifeline, I wrote a letter to televangelist Pat Robertson.

Dear Pat,

I watch your show every day and night when I can. I've put my hands on the TV as you have prayed for everyone. With little to no victory in my life, I'm desperate for help. I've asked Jesus into my life. I read my Bible. But I'm gay and can't seem to change.

I'm considering ending my life so I can stop feeling this constant loneliness and rejection from all sides. If you could help me in any way and pray for me, I would so appreciate it.

Thank you, David Lowry

There...done, I thought, watching the letter fall into the postbox. *I've asked a man for help. No sexual intentions, no abuse—just a man who says he loves me.*

Well, I guess we'll see if that's true.

HINDSIGHT REVELATIONS:
SETTLING FOR OKAY

Increasingly it seems, our culture tends to suggest that "gay is okay." And while I'm not suggesting going to the other extreme and issuing condemnation, I wonder whether this attitude is helpful. Why should sexual preference have anything to do with a person's acceptance one way or the other?

What does okay mean? For some, maybe it carries a sentiment of live and let live—the idea being that what happens between two consensual adults is their own business. For others (perhaps those trying to reconcile the words of the Bible), it might suggest that identifying as gay is okay if the person remains celibate and doesn't allow lust to reign in their thoughts.

In my experience, an okay world left me in limbo, never truly free to move fully into the life God has planned for me.

Whether someone is born gay or not isn't the real issue. God doesn't intend for any of us to stay the way we're naturally born. The Bible says we're being transformed from glory to glory. People can (and should) change. Every one of us. Only Jesus was born perfect.

In fact, all of us inherit generational, genetic, and/or circumstantial challenges to overcome—and change is a positive thing. We don't say "poor is okay" when someone is born into poverty, nor "addict is okay" when someone is born predisposed to an addiction. No matter how we're born, we're encouraged to strive for better than okay.

Some people believe that sexual identity isn't something a person can change, but is more innate like race or gender. Either way, our spirits have neither race nor gender, so these classifications are not part of our true identity. If people are labeled with identifiers such as woman or black or gay, does that tell us who they are as individuals, at the core level? Most personality tests (e.g., Myers–Briggs) don't factor in race, gender, or sexual preference. Why do we hold so tightly to these classifications, even as we struggle to free ourselves of certain stigmas associated with them?

Standing in solidarity with minorities and celebrating diversity can be beautiful things. But are we willing to look beyond this and become part of an even larger tapestry?

Do our preconceived notions and labels limit our capacity to see who God is calling us to be?

Perhaps I still could have lived as a Christian by deciding that God made me gay and that was okay. But in my heart, I knew this wasn't complete freedom. I would never have experienced the joy of feeling whole. Now viewing my struggle from the top of the hill, I'm so glad I forged ahead.

15

WHO CARES?

LATE TWENTIES

THE PHONE RANG and my heart sprang up when I heard Ms. Ruth's voice. It seemed like quite a while since I'd seen her, so I was thrilled by her invitation to lunch and couldn't wait to meet at our usual spot. I'd been feeling a bit better after writing Pat Robertson, but even so, seeing Ms. Ruth would be a needed shot of joy to my system.

She was already waiting for me when I got to the restaurant, looking radiant as always. We small-talked a bit and she asked about my new job. As usual, the conversation quickly turned to the subject of my spiritual growth. We never talked about my sexuality or specific sins. Ms. Ruth was always pointing me forward and helping me see myself the way God saw me. I knew I could tell her anything, but when I was with her, I was inspired to be the best version of myself—my sexuality didn't seem to matter.

"So tell me, kid, what are you and Jesus up to these days?"

"Hmm…guess I've been feeling kinda stuck," I admitted. "You'll probably think this is crazy, but I sent a letter to Pat Robertson asking for help." I decided not mention just how dark things had gotten to drive me to that point.

"Sounds like a great step of faith. Hope God will use it," Ms. Ruth said.

I wasn't so sure about that. Right now, hoping for anything felt uncomfortable.

"I don't know," I said dejectedly. "He's a big TV star. He'll probably let me down like most everyone else."

"Well, you might as well get used to that," she said with a knowing chuckle. "Mankind is always going to disappoint you—I'm sure *I'll* disappoint you one day. Only Jesus is perfect. Even so, you'll probably feel disappointed by him too, when things don't work out how you'd like. The difference is, he's the only one you can ever completely trust. He knows what's best, even when we don't."

I couldn't imagine Ms. Ruth ever letting me down, but I got the gist of what she was saying. And I was sure that I'd done my fair share of disappointing people too. Maybe I used my fear of disappointment as an excuse, blaming others instead of taking responsibility. I sat thoughtfully, digesting this bite by bite, much like the eggroll I was eating.

Somewhat abruptly, a new thought popped into my head. "Oh, almost forgot," I said, "I need to tell you something that I haven't shared with anyone."

"Do tell!" she said with a raised eyebrow, leaning in close. "I had another one of those weird experiences…"

I paused, trying to figure out exactly what I was going to say. A curious smile tugged at the corners of Ms. Ruth's mouth as she motioned for me to go on.

"It happened on the day you taught me about the Holy Spirit. I was just sitting in my living room when…." I continued to share the "beam of light" experience with Ms. Ruth, describing how I was able to sing in another language. "So then Carson came in and not long after, we broke up. Since then, I've kinda been in survival mode, so I haven't thought much more about it. Any idea what that whole thing was about?"

Ms. Ruth shook her head disgustedly. For a second, I was afraid she thought I was making it all up.

"That's just like Satan," she said, pinching her eyebrows together. "He uses whatever tactics he can to distract people from realizing what they've been given. He's been magnifying your pain to hide God's gift from you."

"Gift? What do you mean?"

I didn't remember opening any sort of gift.

"Honey, you got filled with the Holy Ghost! You were given the gift of tongues."

I sat quietly for a while, not knowing what to say. This sounded a little scary.

"*Okay...*" I said tentatively. "So what do I do with it?"

"Just open your mouth and pray, kid. Let the Holy Spirit do his thing. It's powerful!"

I couldn't quite believe it. I felt simultaneously validated and unworthy at the same time. A present from God? For me? That must mean he accepts me. But I'm the gay guy, so how could that be? I wasn't sure what to make of this. Why would God give *me* a gift—one I had no idea how to use?

On the way home, I thought more about everything Ms. Ruth had said. I wished there were more people I could talk to and pray with. Maybe a man. Someone who could relate more closely to what I was going through. Debbie kept saying I needed to find a local church that could be a support network. But I was pretty sure church would be the last place I'd find anybody like me.

I stopped by my mailbox on the way to my apartment. As I stepped inside, sorting through the stack of envelopes, my heart sank. *Will the bills ever stop coming?*

But then, I saw it. The very last letter had a return address from *The 700 Club*. Adrenaline ran through me as I nervously opened the envelope.

"Dear David," it began. Before reading the rest, I hurriedly flipped to the last page to look at the signature. It was hand signed, "Pat." I was shaking in awe as I read his words, "hope...redemption in Christ...a new creation...the church loves you...transformation...yes, we're here to help."

I couldn't believe that a man of such prestige would write *me* a letter. And not a canned letter—but an eight-page, personal letter. If he could take the time to write me and offer such loving hope, then maybe this Christian thing *was* real. Maybe I wasn't crazy. Deep down in the canyon of darkness that surrounded my soul, this letter lit a match of hope. Maybe I really could change.

I called Debbie a few days later. During the course of a long conversation about the letter and my struggles, she asked whether I was worried about AIDS. I wasn't sure where she was going with this.

"Not really," I said. "It's mostly in San Francisco, right?"

I would later lose many friends to AIDS, but it hadn't hit home yet. Even so, whatever Debbie's concerns and good intentions, this was one of those moments when I realized the person I was talking to couldn't relate to me nor the depth of my struggles. It was a very lonely feeling.

After an awkward pause, Debbie must have sensed that I was caught off-guard by her question and reverted to our original subject.

"Why don't you just call some churches and ask if they offer counseling for gay people?" she suggested.

That seemed like a long shot, but I decided it couldn't hurt to try.

I was wrong—it hurt.

I sat on the floor and flipped to the yellow pages in my phone book.

Who first? Guess I'll start with the Presbyterians since that's the church I grew up in.

"Hello, can you tell me if you have any help for gay people?" I asked.

After a long silence, the voice on the other end of the line said, "Um, no. We don't do that here."

"Okay, thank you."

I took a minute to regroup, then dialed another one. "Hello, can you tell me if you have any help for gay people?"

"Oh, we don't let gay people attend here. It's too dangerous...haven't you heard of AIDS?"

Apparently, this was on everyone's mind these days.

Maybe I should watch the news more often.

I tried again.

"Hello, can you tell me if you have any help for gay people?"

"I'm sorry. We don't minister to gays. They're living a very sinful life and are going to hell."

Not sure how many churches I called that day and in the days to come, but not one of them offered help. They all gave various excuses but their responses were similar: uncomfortable, dismissive, and sometimes flat-out hateful. The net result was one of the most painful rejections I'd experienced yet.

I'm officially a leper. If I'm not even welcome among God's people, where can I turn?

Remarkably, these thoughts only momentarily deterred me. A Scripture came to mind, as if someone had handed me a shield to protect me from an onslaught of arrows. I recalled something I'd read in the book of John: "He came to his own people, and even they rejected him."

It was hard to believe that Jesus—*the Son of God*—had been rejected by the religious people of his day. But I knew it was true. And he endured much more than I had. They spit in his face, beat him severely, hung him on a cross, and watched him die as if it were entertainment.

Knowing that Jesus understood what I was going through brought me a measure of comfort and strengthened my resolve to keep going. There had to be *someone* who could help me.

I dialed Emma and caught her up on everything that had been going on since she'd moved.

"David, I'm so sorry you're going through this. And I'm sorry I can't be there for you. My new church family here is praying for you. We believe in you. God's Word is true—you are a new creation in Christ."

Hearing that complete strangers were praying for me moved me to tears.

"So don't give up, okay?" she continued. "I remember hearing about a church in Indy called Faith Church. You should check that one out."

"Emma, I've called almost every church in the yellow pages and pretty much had the receiver slammed in my ear each time."

"I think this one is different—I have a feeling about it. Please try just one more, okay? I know this is hard," she said empathetically. "It's not easy to follow Jesus, but continue to persevere. You'll find a church that loves you like Christ loves you, I promise."

I wished that I felt as sure about that as she did. Of course, she'd been right before. Emma was the one who'd suggested I become a hairdresser when I'd never even thought of it. And that's what had really started this whole journey. Maybe God was speaking to me through Emma. I decided to give Faith a try.

Sunday morning came quickly and the alarm jolted me out of a deep sleep.

Ugh, ten a.m. already? Service starts at eleven—better get moving.

I started the coffee and looked out my window at a depressing view of a dirty street. Chemicals and grime from cars had made a filthy mess out of the once-beautiful snow-fall. The street looked as dirty as I felt inside. I started having second thoughts.

Am I really brave enough to try this church thing in person?

I shuddered, remembering how poorly the phone conversations had gone. Maybe if I cleaned up, on the outside at least, I'd blend in and no one would know.

What do I wear?

When I was a kid everyone wore suits and ties, but I didn't have either one. I opted instead for black pants and a pinstriped button-down shirt, hoping that would suffice. My hands were shaking as I combed my hair. I tried giving myself a pep talk.

It'll be fine. All I have to do is relax and be myself.

Yeah, right, that should go over well.

As I put my blinker on and turned into the church parking lot, I felt a little sick as I saw everyone walking to the front doors in suits and dresses.

Go home. You can't do this.

Yes, I can. Besides, I promised Emma.

I took a deep breath, got out of my car, and put one foot in front of the other.

Okay, Jesus…I'm in front of the doors. Now what?
I sat in the back, hoping no one would notice me. But everyone seemed to take a curious glance at the new person as they walked by. I was pretty sure I had the word "GAY" stamped on my forehead. *Might as well be 666, mark of the beast,* I thought sarcastically.

I wanted to bolt right then, but somehow I managed to get through the entire service. It was fairly uneventful. The pastor seemed nice enough (although I didn't actually talk to him). I didn't burst into flames, so that was a plus. But I didn't feel anything change. I didn't feel much at all, really. And no one talked to me, which I decided was probably for the best.

I cried on the way home, praying and aching inside for a miraculous event to take place. But nothing happened.

A few weeks passed. I continued to show up at church, though I had to talk myself into going each time. One Sunday morning, that heavy darkness seemed to be hovering around again. I'd been at this Christian thing for three years now and it seemed to result in more heartache than help. In a moment of weakness, I was ready to throw in the towel.

Instead of getting ready for church, I climbed back into bed.

Not a minute later, the phone rang. I reached over to grab it off the nightstand.

"Hello?" I mumbled. It was Emma.

"Hey, David!" she said in her sunny voice. I usually loved her positivity, but found it irritating this morning. "I was calling to check in on you. See how you like Faith."

"I don't know. It's okay," I said. "I like Pastor Dan, but the people seem…different. I don't fit in and I'm not sure they can help me."

Emma said she and her church would keep praying for me. I hung up, sighed, and dragged myself out of bed.

I couldn't go on this way anymore. My world had been turned upside down. And for what? Nothing makes sense. Everything seems to be getting worse instead of better.

Looking in the mirror, I made a deal with myself.

This is it. If I don't get something out of church today, it's over.

With that, I scraped together every ounce of hope and strength I had left and headed off to church for one last Hail Mary pass.

I sat in my now-usual spot in the back. I didn't get as many stares these days, but no one talked to me either. I always tried to avoid eye contact, so that probably didn't help matters.

Pastor Dan spoke on the love of God the Father. This intrigued me. God, as a loving father? What does that look like? This had never been my experience. I knew the Scripture that said, "God so loved the world…" and I guess that included me. But I'd never been able to personalize it. I couldn't feel his love, only his disappointment.

Why is that?

We stood up for the last song. I glanced up and became captivated by one of the women singing in the choir. Our eyes met. She smiled at me and I realized that she reminded me of my mother. I wondered what Mom was singing this morning at her church.

I heard the congregation singing, "Great is thy faithfulness. Great is thy faithfulness," but now it sounded like there was a multitude of voices joining in. I felt a sense of connection.

The song ended and before I could turn to get out of my pew, a hand touched my shoulder. The touch was gentle, but conveyed a sense of strength and comfort. My eyes followed the hand—translucent with age and knotted by arthritis—to its owner. She must have been ninety, but was positively striking. Silver-white hair. Sparkling blue eyes. You could see the young person inside of her.

"Young man, I'm so happy you came here today," she said. "My name is Liz."

Without hesitation, I introduced myself in return. "I'm David."

"Sure glad to meet you, David. Now you go and have a wonderful day."

She smiled in a way that warmed me from the inside out. "Likewise…you too," I said, looking down to realize we were holding hands.

Then she walked down the aisle and disappeared into the crowd.

Did she know about me? Was she real? She touched me. She wasn't afraid. What was that feeling?

It felt like someone cared. It felt like love.

What happened that Sunday morning shifted my perspective about church. The encounter with Liz. The angelic choir lady who'd smiled at me. The connection I'd felt with my mother, the congregation, and maybe even angels in heaven, as we all sang together. And the message about the love of God the Father, which for a brief moment, didn't seem so far-fetched.

I'd been a lonely castaway, shipwrecked on an island. But someone had air-dropped a few packages of food. It was enough, spiritually, to keep me going. I remembered what Ms. Ruth had said about the good gifts of God. These had been simple things—kindness, gentleness, love. This had been my first taste of feeling connected to a body of believers.

HINDSIGHT REVELATIONS: THE CHURCH'S RESPONSE

The church's response to people who identify themselves as gay typically falls into one of two categories:

1) Churches who use the Bible to condemn and shun people living alternative sexual lifestyles.
2) Churches who interpret the Bible loosely and affirm people's sexual lifestyles, whether or not they hope to change.

Of course, there are also many shades in between these extremes.

Some people simply have no idea what to think or how to respond.

Unfortunately, those who are struggling with sin of any kind are often dismissed right off the bat by the church. In other cases, they might be welcomed or tolerated. But few churches know how to actually walk with people through a gentle—often slow—process of transformation.

Sometimes, fear or pride clouds the way Christians think and respond. Other times, people feel exasperated when they don't know how to help or don't see change quickly enough. It's tempting to sidestep what we don't understand and it's easy to give up.

Sin is messy business. Relationships are messy. But love transcends everything. My hope would be to see the church open its arms lovingly to welcome people—then not be afraid to walk with them and stick by them through hard times. We can trust God with the process. If a person truly wants to change, the Holy Spirit will do the work. There's not a plan or formula to follow; it's the love of Christ that changes hearts.

In my case, I endured a lot of rejection and could have easily given up many times. But God used people like Emma and even Pat Robertson (who has been known to take a very conservative stance on homosexuality), to offer me hope and provide the encouragement that change was indeed possible.

16

DEEPER STILL

LATE TWENTIES

I FILLED OUT a prayer request card at church. Didn't go into details, but simply told them I was gay and needed help. My phone rang the very next day. The man introduced himself as Stephen, one of the elders of the church. He asked if we could meet in person. I immediately said yes, not quite believing this was really happening. Someone from a church actually wanted to help me?

A few hours later, my doorbell rang. I turned the knob with the same sense of trepidation you might have when opening the door for a blind date.

What am I about to get into?

Stephen said hello with a broad grin spreading across his face as he shook my hand. I was surprised to see that he wasn't super old, like I expected a church "elder" to be. He was forty, tops, with a full head of wavy brown hair and warm eyes. His friendly manner immediately put me at ease.

I poured Stephen some water while he explained his relationship with the church and told me a bit of his personal story.

"But I didn't come here to talk about me," Stephen said. "You asked for help, so I'm here to listen."

I sat in silence for a few seconds, not sure where or how to begin.

"Well…" I finally said, "in a nutshell, I'm gay." I waited for him to say something in response. He simply nodded, so I continued. "But the way I understand the Bible, that's not the way Jesus wants me to live, so I'm trying to figure out how to change. I ended things with my boyfriend, but I'm still attracted to men."

I held my breath as I awaited his response. I wondered which one of the stock answers I'd get. Would he say I should accept the way God made me, but remain celibate? Or would he go to the other extreme and tell me I was going to burn in hell?

I was floored to hear a completely different reaction.

"Boy, that's gotta be tough, David," he said. "I've never had to deal with that particular sin…but I've got my own sins, so I know how hard it can feel to change old patterns of thinking and behaving. But all things are possible with God. The answer is always the same for me. Jesus paid the price for all of our sins…past, present, and future."

I was relieved he wasn't condemning me to hell or placating me, but he didn't answer my real question: *How the heck do I change?*

I already knew Jesus died for me. That hadn't helped change my desires. And maybe Stephen had sins, but I doubted they were anything like mine. I bet his sin wasn't thrown in his face every single day. I couldn't simply avoid all men in general—not to mention the shirtless men jogging along the canal and handsome gay men at the salon.

I felt sad and frustrated, but I knew Stephen was trying to help.

That was more than most people were willing to do.

"Thanks, Stephen." I said. "I agree with you…and I'm grateful for all that Jesus has done for me. But it doesn't seem to make a dent in my temptation level."

Stephen nodded and looked thoughtful.

"Tell ya what," he said. "Let me pray about this and we'll be in touch."

As I shut the door, I immediately regretted exposing my secret to the church.

WE'LL be in touch? Great, now other people were getting involved. How was I going to show my face at church again?

That Friday night I found myself back at the bars, feeling hopeless again, looking for any possibility of love. I cried all the way there, apologizing to God.

Sorry, I can't help it. I have to go.

I noticed something different on this particular night. I was standing at the bar, and when I looked around, I saw a perfect semicircle of empty space separating me from any other men in the bar. It was as if there was a force field or a hedge of protection keeping us apart. I wondered if there was a circle of angels surrounding me.

It was like Jesus was saying, "I'm not going to let this happen." I could feel his love for me.

"Okay," I said under my breath. "I get it. I choose you."

I walked out, making a pledge that I would never go back to a gay bar again. And I never have. This wasn't the end of my struggles, but it was a huge tipping point.

After a lot of prayer, I summoned up the courage to go to church the following Sunday. Thankfully, I didn't notice anyone whispering or pointing, so I thought I was in the clear and Stephen hadn't told anyone my secret. Pastor Dan greeted me as I was leaving. He asked if I would like to have coffee sometime, so we arranged a meeting. As I got in my car, I felt that same uncomfortable feeling of exposure.

He knows...I'm sure of it.

A few days later, Pastor Dan sipped coffee and listened intently as I spilled my guts. I surveyed his deep blue eyes. He looked friendly enough, but I worried what kind of judgment he was about to pronounce.

"David, I have never met anyone like you," he said. "Nor do we have anyone in our church who has knowledge or experience with the specific challenges you're facing. But if you'd like, I can walk this out with you. I'll try to understand and do whatever I can to help. What would you think about meeting every Tuesday for breakfast at 7:00 a.m.?"

So that's what we did. Over time, we developed a deep relationship. Pastor Dan admitted he had no idea what to do but love me. In so many ways, that was what I needed most.

I suppose word travels fast in a church environment, especially about someone like me. I got the sense that I was like an exotic bird or some kind of endangered species that they were determined to protect. "Look who we got…a struggling gay guy!" It felt a little strange to be suddenly famous—or infamous—because my sin happened to be different from everyone else's, but most people meant well and treated me with kindness. Of course, there were a few who wouldn't give me the time of day; but overwhelmingly, this body of believers welcomed me with open arms. Warts and all.

I began to feel a true sense of community, something I'd never experienced in a church. Hugs and smiles and friendship. In spite of this, my identity and label was still "gay" and my sexual appetite didn't lighten up. I decided I needed to find someone with experience in these matters.

In his letter, Pat Robertson had listed some resources, including an "ex-gay" ministry in California. I called the number and learned there was going to be a conference in Baltimore that focused on same-sex attraction. I was excited about this—until I tallied up all of the costs. I still had loans and bills to pay. There was no way I could come up with the extra money *and* take an entire week off work. I didn't want to go further in debt, so I decided to table it until I was on top of my finances.

When I arrived at the salon the following morning, I looked through my schedule and prepared for the day ahead. One of my favorite clients was due in soon, which gave my spirits an instant lift. Joanie was a lovely spitfire of a red-head, and very forthcoming about her faith. I'd discovered right out of the gate that she was Catholic. At first, I wasn't sure how that would play out since I'd learned that having a shared Christian faith didn't necessarily mean you believed the same things. But in her case, it didn't seem to matter. We both loved Jesus and that was that. Our conversations were somehow deep and easygoing at the same time.

Joanie was a friend of Stephen's, so I felt safe opening up to her. We mutually shared our troubles and triumphs with each other while I cut and colored her hair. I felt blessed to have the luxury of developing personal relationships with my clients.

That was one of the things I loved so much about being a hairstylist. It had the same backbone of serving people that the restaurant business did, with the added bonus of really getting to know people and helping them feel renewed when they walked out the door. I came to find that my beauty chair could be like a therapy chair. It felt like the Holy Spirt often put people in my chair so I could help them, even just by listening—and sometimes he put people in my chair to help me.

As Joanie and I chatted, I told her everything that had been going on and mentioned the conference in Baltimore. I told her even though I couldn't go, I was glad to know such a thing existed so I could start saving.

The next week, Joanie came in with a funny sort of smile on her face. She ceremoniously sat down in my chair, then suddenly looked very serious.

"Everything okay, Joanie? You look like you're about to lay something heavy on me."

"You could say that," she said. "Here's the deal. I'm about to tell you something that's between me and Jesus. It involves you too, but it's my act of obedience—so don't try turning me down, ya hear?" She winked as she said this last bit.

"Um, okay…I guess." I had no idea where this was going.

"David, I think Jesus wants you to go to Baltimore." She paused dramatically before continuing. "So I'm going to pay for all of it—conference, airfare, hotel. Plus a little extra to cover your time off work. It's a gift, no strings attached."

A river of gratitude flowed from deep inside me, causing tears to stream down my face as I hugged Joanie, unable to form words. I was truly humbled. Her obedience, as she'd called it, was an answer to my prayers. Finally, I could get the help I needed. For the first time in a long while, I dared to hope that I could be healed.

I was nervous walking into the conference, not knowing what to expect. My first reaction was sheer awe at how many people were there. Probably 150 men and women of different ages, all dealing with same-sex attraction and looking for support. I could barely wrap my head around the fact that I wasn't alone in this struggle.

We gathered together to hear people share their stories of walking away from "the lifestyle" and leading godly lives.

These testimonies were hugely encouraging. I was deeply intrigued by the fact that these people no longer identified themselves as gay. But I still worried that I would not get to experience this. It seemed too good to be true. Could I ever really be free? My heart remained guarded.

Even by the end of the week, I was still hesitant to be transparent and make connections. I felt like a remedial student who didn't fully grasp my new identity or understand who I was in Christ. These teachings were still new to me. What did it mean to be "in Christ"? How did that change anything? I wished there were some practical steps I could take. This all seemed like a big mind game that I couldn't win.

Familiar questions resurfaced. It had taken me years to conclude that I was indeed gay. Would it now take even longer to accept that I *wasn't* gay (or so I was being told)? Why was so much of my identity tangled up in my sexuality? The harder I tried to turn away from these desires, the more I thought about them, the more they consumed me.

On the final morning of the conference, I walked around outside with a heart that was literally aching with such intense pain that I thought I might be dying.

Am I having a heart attack?

Don't be stupid…you're only in your twenties.

Then why does it hurt so much?

Because you're a broken loser, beyond help and beyond hope.

Jesus…please. You can help me, can't you? I'm begging you to fix me. I don't want to live this way. I CAN'T live this way. Please do something! Why won't you help me?

I went back to my room, flopped on my bed, and cried myself dry. After lying there a minute more, something inside me wouldn't let me give up. Mother always said I was bull-headed. I guess in this instance that served me well.

I decided to go find Robert Frost, one of the conference speakers whose story had especially touched me. Surprisingly, he wasn't hard to track down. The people at his book table said he was always happy to talk with people and they gave me his room number. I probably should have called first, but instead walked straight to his room before I lost my nerve.

My heart was beating double time as I stood at his door, waiting for him to answer my knock. He opened the door with a smile, almost as if he'd been expecting me.

"Hi Robert…I'm David," I said, unconsciously letting out a big sigh. "I'm so sorry to bother you, but I've tried everything and everyone. I don't know where else to turn."

My tear ducts had called in reinforcements and pools of salty water were right at the surface again.

"Come in, David," he said, gesturing for me to sit on the couch in his suite.

We talked for a bit and I explained the reason for my heartache. He was a man of action and said we should get right to the heart of it. He wanted to try something that, in those days, was called inner healing. I said I was willing to try anything.

"We're going to start by unraveling your past. Tell me about your relationship with your father."

"Okay…" I took a deep breath. "Well, there's not a lot to tell. Growing up, my dad was a pretty unemotional man. That's how men were supposed to be on the farm. Stoic and detached. But I never could seem to get that down pat. It's how my grandfather was too—although he showed anger if you weren't on his good side."

"No man is unemotional." Robert looked me square in the eyes to make sure his words were connecting. "By nature, humans are emotional creatures. Now, some men may try to hide their emotions. They might even stuff them down deep enough to convince themselves they don't feel anything. But that's a lie."

He paused a minute, giving me time to process this.

"Your dad probably didn't show his emotions because that's the way his father was with him. He'd never learned to relate to other men in that way. David, you've actually been given a gift in *not* being able to detach from your emotions. You can break the generational pattern in your family."

I'd never seen it that way, but now that he explained it, everything started to make some sense. A memory popped into my mind from my grandmother's funeral, just a few years back.

Everyone went to their cars after the burial. Mom told me that Dad had stayed at the casket, so I went back to check on him. I was astonished to find that he was crying—I'd never seen him show emotion like this. I put my hand gently on his shoulder and said, "Dad, it's time to go."

Then he hugged me for the first time in my life. I found it especially remarkable because it genuinely felt like a pure expression of love. And he wasn't reaching out to meet his needs, but instead he was trying to meet mine. Something shifted between us in that moment, but of course, we didn't say a word to each other about our feelings.

I'd only seen Dad a handful of times since that day, so we hadn't had the chance to build on that hug. Everything pretty much went back to how it had always been.

Sitting in Robert's hotel room now, the revelation that my dad had real emotions after all helped me receive that hug on a deeper level. I let the truth about my father's love for me penetrate the walls of my heart. Taking all of this in, I experienced major healing that day. I wept tears of regret for the pain of the past.

These turned into tears of joy as I was filled with new hope for the future. Jesus had applied his healing power of love and forgiveness, like bandages to my wounded heart.

But he wasn't done with me yet.

Back home, I started to put some of the things I'd learned into practice. If I wanted true wholeness, I was going to have to make some difficult choices. For starters, I kept my pledge to stay out of gay bars and decided to stay out of *any* bars until I felt stronger. I couldn't avoid seeing attractive men in my daily life, but I could at least avoid the toxic combination of drinking and being in an atmosphere where people were looking to hook up. Instead, I needed to spend more time refreshing my mind and discovering God's thoughts and plans for me as I read the Bible. So that's what I did, both on my own and with men from church.

I was amazed to find that my heart and desires really did begin to change.

HINDSIGHT REVELATIONS: THE CHOICE

Perhaps the hardest part about changing is deciding—truly deciding—to embrace the change. For a long time, I'd been sincere about wanting to change, but was still clinging to comforts and habits of the past. The Holy Spirit couldn't do his work in my life until I wholeheartedly invited and allowed him to do so. When I finally let go, he began to change my heart, replacing lies with truth. And this changed my desires. Ultimately, I wanted what God wanted.

Our desires aren't all bad. In a way, they can actually be clues to point us toward the life God has for us. Temptations of the flesh present a shortcut to get what our hearts truly desire. In my case, intimacy with men had proven to be an enticing way to experience feelings of love and fulfillment. But I started to realize this was only a glimpse of the kind of pure love and satisfaction that Jesus offered. I had been like a child playing with a rusty old toy who wouldn't put it down to pick up the shiny new gift at his feet.

None of this was easy. Deciding to change and to let go of that old toy, incited an epic battle within me. It was Self vs. Spirit, fighting it out in a boxing ring, round after round after round. One day, I realized that we all serve somebody. It's a question of who that's going to be. Was I going to serve:

Myself—by giving in to temptation?

The world—by focusing on temporary pursuits? The devil—by believing his lies?

Or Jesus—by trusting in his promise of abundant, eternal life?

As I considered my choices, I realized that only one of these offered anything genuine, lasting, and truly satisfying. Only one always had my best interests at heart. Only one loved me so much that he died for me.

So I chose Jesus. And then I chose him over and over again, each time I was tempted to serve anyone or anything else.

17

A LITTLE HELP FROM MY FRIENDS

LATE TWENTIES

COMING together with friends from church to pray and read the Bible helped protect me like a suit of armor during this vulnerable time. There was still a battle going on, no doubt about it. But I was determined and strengthened by God's truth as it continued to nourish my mind and heart.

Even so, I still felt a void, no matter how much I went to church. Plain and simple, I was lonely. For so long, I had pinned so much hope on finding the right relationship to fulfill my desire to love and be loved. Now I wasn't sure what to do with myself. I was still learning. Still on guard with my new Christian family. There was part of me that worried about getting in too deep.

They were all so nice to me—for no reason I could discern. Sometimes this would create a fear that maybe I'd unknowingly fallen into a cult (as I'm sure Carson would have suggested), but I knew it was a silly thought. Pastor Dan seemed pretty legit and he wasn't asking me to do anything weird. We mostly just hung out and talked, like friends do.

I'd been following through on my commitment to stay away from the bars, but I did occasionally attend work parties. They were a lot of fun—music, dancing, drinks. At one such party, I noticed that a tall man with animated mannerisms had corralled a group of people. Everyone was doubled over with laughter.

Who is this guy? And why am I the only one who doesn't know him?

I was instantly drawn to him and watched for an opportunity to introduce myself.

"Hey, I'm David," I said, extending my hand.

"Louie. Good to meet ya, David," he said, pumping my arm up and down with an enthusiastic handshake.

"Haven't seen you at one of these things before. What do you do?" I asked.

"I'm in sales. You?"

"Hairdresser," I said. Maybe I imagined it, but I think I saw a funny look flash across his face. *Probably assumes I'm gay and thinks I'm hitting on him.*

"Well, man, I need to get going," he said. "I've had too much to drink and need to make it to church in the morning."

"Yeah, I probably need to do the same. Nice meeting you, Louie."

On the drive home, I wondered about Louie. He said he had church in the morning. But here he was hanging out and partying, having fun like a regular guy. Somewhere along the way, I'd picked up this notion that "good" Christians didn't do anything but go to church and read the Bible. Maybe attend a potluck or something if they were getting really wild. Louie had a different vibe. He was funny and felt like someone I could relate to. I didn't think he was gay, so that was a plus for me. I certainly didn't need the temptation. I'd been praying that the Lord would send me a true friend that I felt I could be myself around. Was Louie my answer? Probably a long shot, but I was intrigued by the possibility.

A few weeks later, Stephen called to invite me to a men's Bible study. I instantly agreed, but regretted being so hasty when I found out they met for breakfast first, at 7:30 a.m. on Saturdays.

Ugh…what are we, roosters?

Tell him you can't. Make an excuse.

Oh sure, just lie to the deacon? No, I need to just suck it up and do it. What've I got to lose?

Sweet, precious sleep, that's what.

It's too late—I already said I'd go so I'll just give it a shot.

Saturday came around quickly. When my alarm went off at six thirty, I had the same argument with myself all over again. Reluctantly, I got out of bed, loaded up with coffee, and headed out the door.

When I walked into the church hall, I was overwhelmed to see a full house. I didn't expect there to be so many men that would get up this early for a Bible study.

What am I gonna say to these people?

Stephen took me around the room, making introductions. Most of the men were much older than I was. I wondered what we could possibly have in common. Finally, I saw a face I recognized.

Pastor Dan welcomed me with a big hug. "Morning, David. So glad you could come."

I filed through the breakfast line, balancing my plate with one hand and stacking pancakes with the other. As I reached for the syrup, another hand grabbed for it at the same time. Reflexively, I pulled away with an apologetic, "Sorry, go ahead." I looked up and was stunned to see that the hand belonged to Louie.

"What are you doing here?" we said simultaneously, laughing at our continued outpouring of awkwardness. The last time we had seen each other we'd been indulging in cocktails, and now, here we were at a Bible study. It felt like we had an inside secret. I was relieved that I wasn't the only one here who didn't seem perfect. That sure felt nice for a change.

As the study progressed, I was able to relax—Louie and I both seemed to be soaking it all in. I was glad I'd pushed through my doubts and sleepiness to attend. I had no idea that God was in the works of forming a friendship that would grow and thrive for decades to come.

The following week was tough for some reason. It always seemed that if I started to make progress, something would rise up to derail it. I usually felt fine when I was with people, but alone in my apartment, doubts and fears would try to crowd back in. I decided to call Emma.

"I just don't get it," I confided. "Why can't I move past this? I've done everything I know to do. Why does it still hurt so much? People at work say I'm in denial. And people at Faith are a mixed bag. Some are cool, but a few weeks ago, I noticed some guys at church whispering when I went by. Where's Jesus, Emma? He doesn't seem to show up anymore. I think the King has left the building."

Emma laughed graciously at my feeble attempt at humor. "No, he's there David. I promise. Even when you can't see or feel him. That's the walk of faith, right?"

Emma paused for a minute and I realized she was waiting for a response.

"Yeah, okay. I know you're right," I agreed. "I just feel so lonely."

"I hear ya. I know this isn't easy," Emma said. "I'm really sorry people can be so hurtful. And I'm sorry you feel alone. But remember that's not true. You know you have an enemy, right? He doesn't want you to feel or see any freedom, so watch out for his lies."

"Tell me about it. I'm so tired of feeling these heavy forces working against me. It's exhausting."

"Hang in there, my friend—you can do this," Emma assured me. "Change usually takes time. It isn't something you wave a magic wand over. Tell you what…can you come down to Atlanta and meet with my pastor? I think he might be able to help."

Willing to give just about anything a try, I booked the flight as soon as I hung up the phone.

Sitting at Emma's kitchen table, a gentle Georgia breeze blew through the window. I tried to relax and enjoy the smells of the wonderful lunch Emma was preparing, but I was wound up pretty tight.

"So when's Pastor Joey getting here?" I asked, nervously drumming my fingers on the table.

Emma smiled and put her hand on mine.

"Any minute. Don't worry, David. He wants to help. We're for you, not against."

I took a deep breath and let it out slowly. I hated this. Even though Pastor Joey already knew some of my history, it was never fun to talk about, especially with strangers. But if he could help, I guess it would be worth it.

Pastor Joey arrived with a big smile and an even bigger hug. I wasn't used to being greeted so enthusiastically by a stranger, much less a pastor. But it went a long way to put me at ease. The food was comforting and offered a nice distraction, so that helped too. We all sat at the table as friends, so I took a stab at opening up.

"Pastor Joey, I know Emma has told you what I'm going through. Can you help me?"

I instantly felt a bit shy after asking. I avoided eye contact, acting as if I was intently concentrated on spearing asparagus with my fork. Although he was very friendly, the pastor had a commanding presence. He was a huge, impressively handsome man. And he was in charge of a big church, which was intimidating. Emma said they spoke in tongues, which was something I hadn't explored much. Even though Ms. Ruth had called this a gift, it kinda freaked me out. To my knowledge, no one at my new church spoke in tongues. I wondered if Pastor Joey had some sort of special connection to the Holy Spirit. Maybe he could lay hands on me and I'd be healed? I felt for sure this was it.

This has to be it.

"Tell me more about what you're hoping for," Pastor Joey coaxed, as if reading my mind but wanting me to confirm it out loud.

I spilled my guts, sharing the story of how I'd accepted Jesus into my life and listing everything I'd done in the hope of changing.

"But it seems that no matter what I do, I'm still attracted to men. I avoid putting myself in the path of temptation. And I'm not feeding or acting on my sexual desires. Sometimes they let up, but they won't go away. I worry that I'll never be truly free."

I could tell the pastor had been listening intently. He sat quietly, pondering all I had said. The words he was about to speak would stick with me from that moment on. At first, they stung, like salt poured over an open wound. But they wound up being sweeter than honey.

"Let me give it to you straight, okay? As I listened to your story and heard you describe where you're at in your walk with Jesus, I had several thoughts…" He paused, leaving me on the edge of my seat. "The sad truth is that many

Christians would say you're not saved, that you're going to hell, end of story."

The gravity of his words sent my heart plummeting into my stomach. My head suddenly weighed more than my neck could handle. I mustered every ounce of strength I had to lift it and fight back the tears that were burning my eyes, trying to claw their way out. My greatest fear was being confirmed. The condemning TV evangelists and churches that had rejected me had been right all along. The pain of the past three years had been for nothing. I was beyond saving. Beyond changing. Beyond hope.

Pastor Joey leaned in close. He grabbed my hands and looked me directly in the eyes.

"I want you to hear me well. David, those people are wrong.

You *are* saved."

I exhaled, not realizing I'd been holding my breath. Every tension in me released. Salty streams of relief and gratitude rolled down my cheeks as he continued.

"You may not be able to see how it's going to pan out, but I can see one thing for certain. You have a repentant heart and great love for Jesus. I want to pray with you now. We're going to ask for healing, for these strongholds to be broken."

As he prayed over me, I felt another layer of weight lifting off my being.

This meeting had renewed my hope at a crucial hour when I'd had only a few crumbs left. I couldn't visibly see the hand of God at work, but he had used Pastor Joey's hands as his own.

The next day, I settled into my seat on the flight home. I looked around at all of the people coming and going, wondering what each of them might be going through. Some of them looked happy, some sad, some indifferent. I realized we all had a common destination, even though we were on different journeys. And we all trusted the pilot to get us where we needed to go.

For the next couple of hours, life seemed suspended. I wished I could stay up there, just watching the clouds, trusting the pilot. Everything seemed okay, peaceful. I decided that I would try to live with that same sort of mentality every day. I would trust Jesus to get me where I needed to go. Maybe my life wasn't a direct flight—but one day, I would arrive.

The following Saturday at Bible study, Louie and I grabbed seats by each other. We chatted a bit as everything was winding up and made plans to grab a bite later that evening. We had a great dinner, complete with lots of laughter. I couldn't help marveling at the fact that my feelings for Louie were purely platonic, even though he was quite handsome. I became more and more certain that he was the friend I'd been praying for.

Back at my house after dinner, the conversation turned more serious.

"So how was your trip to Atlanta?" Louie asked.

"It was good," I said. "Got some stuff worked out…but it's a long haul."

I proceeded to tell Louie the whole story.

"Well there it is, Louie—all of my junk, right on the table. Go ahead, dissect it."

Louie laughed his big, deep laugh.

"No, thanks, got my own pile to dig through." He sat thoughtfully for a minute.

"We're not so different, you know," he concluded. "Different sins maybe, but we've both given our lives to

Jesus and want to please God. Maybe we can walk this out together?"

Louie then took his turn, openly sharing his struggles with me. I was amazed by how easy it was for me to know—beyond a doubt—that Jesus loved him, no matter what. Seeing this so clearly helped me receive that truth more deeply for myself. This sort of mutual revelation became a recurring event for each of us that would lead us down roads of remarkable discovery.

My enduring, unconditional friendship with Louie continues to be one of the greatest gifts God has given me. This special relationship became the catalyst that brought me into a ring of people that God would later use in a way none of us could have imagined.

I gave Jesus the pilot controls and buckled up for quite a ride.

HINDSIGHT REVELATIONS: OBEDIENCE

A dear friend once told me, "David, don't waste your pain." I didn't fully understand what this meant at the time, but I think I do now. No one likes pain nor wishes for it, but God can—and does—use it for good. To teach us. To help us grow. And to help others. In fact, that's why I've written this book. I'm determined that my pain will not go to waste.

There's usually some measure of pain involved in learning to follow Jesus. It may not sound like fun, but obedience—whether to Scripture or prompts of the Holy Spirit—yields rich rewards. For instance, my obedience in getting up early for the Saturday morning Bible study led to my friendship with Louie. It's like the exercise motto "no pain, no gain." My mind, body, soul, and spirit are connected. Obedience is like exercise for my soul, bringing my whole being in line with my spirit. This is how I'm best able to connect with God.

Obedience often requires sacrifice or surrender. There's typically a battle in my mind as to whether or not I will follow through. When I want to give in or give up, it helps me to look past the immediate moment. What are my motivations? What are the likely outcomes? Will my actions yield lasting peace and/or joy? The more resistance I meet, the more I've learned to suspect it is worth the fight. There are forces working against our obedience, but there's an even more powerful force helping us push through. With every victory, we are transformed.

Obedience to God may *sound* restrictive, but counter-intuitively, it leads to greater freedom. For instance, I toyed with quitting smoking for years but wasn't able to give it up until it became a matter of obedience for me. Merely wanting to quit wasn't enough to make me want to give it up. I both wanted to quit and wanted the next cigarette.

I could have chased my tail for years. When I decided to honor my body in order to honor God, something was different. Cigarettes tasted bitter. I didn't want one anymore.

This bitterness served a purpose, just as pain often does. Whether pain comes to us through our own decisions or from another source, God can put it to work for us—especially if we take a posture of obedience. Pain can help us move beyond our desire for earthly comforts and into the deeper delights of God.

18

TRUTH OR DARE

THIRTIES

PERSEVERANCE finally paid off as a storybook world began to unfold before my very eyes. I'd emerged from the haunted forest with true friends at my side, and could see Oz gleaming straight ahead.

Life was exciting and scary at the same time. I was learning a completely new way of thinking and beginning to walk in the truth of who I really was in God's eyes. This reality was still mysterious and difficult to grasp at times, but it made a profound impact on me. I felt a deep sense of belonging.

It was a good thing that my spiritual life was keeping me firmly rooted. I needed that balance because my career began taking off, potentially luring me in worldly directions. I went from a rented chair in a small shop to owning my own salon. I felt renewed, even strong, as I ventured further into what surely seemed to be the Promised Land. Affluent customers encouraged me to even higher aspirations and drew me into the world of fashion. Glitz, glamour, and travel made up the fabric of my new lifestyle. I was exposed to jaw-dropping extravagance and wealth far beyond anything a little farm boy could ever have imagined. My dreams were coming true and I was mindful to give all the credit to God.

It was an exciting time, for sure. Investing my time at church continued to bless me with new friendships and new revelations from the Bible. Louie and I continued to meet regularly. I really felt like I'd found my place and my people. To the watching world, it probably seemed that I had it all. But alone at home, I spent most nights on my knees, asking God for a wife and family. I started thinking about pursuing a relationship with a woman—if the right one came along.

As it turned out, I didn't have to wait too long. A coworker pulled me aside in the breakroom one day with a proposal.

"Hey, David…any interest in going out with Tracy?" she asked, raising her eyebrows suggestively.

Hmmm, a date? Holding hands? Maybe even kissing?

Though I'd been hoping to move in this direction, the actual possibility of going out with a woman seemed foreign and frightening to me. After all, things hadn't panned out so well with Jill—or any of my romantic relationships for that matter. Did I dare trust someone again?

But rising up over my fear, a newfound sense of masculinity seemed to overpower my old ways of thinking. I no longer embraced homosexuality as my identity. A feeling of wholeness emboldened me. It reminded me of the sense of freedom I'd enjoyed as a young boy, riding wild ponies with my lasso at my side. I was ready to tackle this challenge.

Besides, I liked Tracy. Our paths had crossed at various social gatherings. She was cute and spunky. At the very least, I thought we might have fun.

"Okay, I'll ask her out," I said. "But if she's just wanting to hook up, that's not going to happen. Probably best to have that out there."

"Noted," my friend laughed. "Let's double date. We can act as a buffer in case you don't hit it off…or in case you *do* hit it off," she added with a wink.

"Sounds like a plan," I said, relieved by this suggestion.

Turns out "hit it off" was an understatement. I fell for Tracy in a big way. Not only did I like her personality, but I was attracted to her physically as well. This was different from the heady, superficial attractions I'd experienced in the past. I had a sense of peace about being with her—I'd never experienced this when dating before. I was doing this God's way, and it felt right for the first time.

Tracy and I had an amazing time together and quickly became inseparable. My emotions were flying fast and high like a 747, yet I was determined to stay grounded. The past kept haunting me. If I wanted to build this relationship on a godly foundation, I knew I needed to tell Tracy the truth sooner rather than later.

One night, as we walked along the canal after a lovely dinner, I mustered up the courage to be open with her.

"Tracy, I need to share some stuff with you," I said, tentatively. "It might make you uneasy. But I've got to be totally honest with you." Tracy made an exaggerated "eek" face and crossed her eyes.

Her sense of humor was one of the things I really loved about her.

"C'mon, I'm serious."

"Okay, lay it on me," she said, pretending to wipe the smile off her face. "What is it? Some dark, secret life? Murderer? Ex-con? I can handle it."

She was still trying to make light of the situation, but I noticed her take a deep breath.

Well...here goes, Jesus. I'm about to filet myself with this girl.

Help me out here?

"First of all, I gave my life to Jesus awhile back…" The first several words felt stuck in my mouth, but once I got that much out, the rest poured out like captives who found an escape route. "And he totally changed my life. I'd been involved in a gay lifestyle—but now I'm not. That's in the past, and…"

I stopped, needing to take a breath and gauge her reaction. She seemed deep in thought, but I had no idea what was going on in her head.

"Look, Tracy," I continued with a sigh, afraid this wasn't going well. "I really like you. But I've learned the hard way that our relationship will never work unless we both believe in Jesus. So I need to know how you feel about that. And about my past too, I guess."

Tracy didn't say anything. I almost started talking again to fill in the space, but as soon as I opened my mouth, she broke her silence.

"Wow, okay. That's…a lot," she said, fiddling with her necklace. A slight smile broke across her face. "Glad to hear you're not a murderer. I'm not much for blood." She scrunched her nose to emphasize the point.

"Tracy—"

"I know, I know—you're serious," she said, regrouping. "I don't really know what to say. I mean, I'm not super religious, so I don't know about going all-in on the Jesus thing. But I really like you too, so I'll try to keep an open mind."

I was glad to hear this, but still waiting for the bomb to drop.

She looked thoughtful again.

"Gay, huh?" she raised an eyebrow. "But now you're not?" I nodded. She shrugged in response.

"Well, I only know who you are now…and he's pretty great. So if you say you've changed, your past doesn't really

COMING OUT

matter to me." I could hardly believe what I was hearing. I
couldn't speak, so I just nodded again. It was all I could do to
hold back tears of joy.

Driving home that night with Tracy holding my hand,
I felt amazing. Her acceptance of me, even after everything
I'd told her, brought a deep peace to my soul. Better still, she
was willing to learn about Jesus.
Could this be the one?
Another thought slid in behind that one.
*C'mon, you're just faking all of this to try and prove to
yourself and the world that you're not gay.*
Shut up.
You know it's true.
*No—I know it's a lie. I belong to Jesus. That old life is
gone. I'm a new person.*
Having quoted Scripture, I was surprised to find that
my negative thoughts were quieted. I went back to enjoying
the moment, now feeling quite victorious.

As the weeks went by, my relationship with Tracy continued to flourish. I was anxious to bring Jesus into the conversation, but didn't want it to feel forced. Should I suggest
that we read the Bible together? Pray together? I was having
trouble finding a natural opening.
Some friends came to the rescue. Dave and his wife,
Penny, were youth pastors—the cool couple at church. Dave
and I had found a connection after discovering that we grew
up just forty-five minutes from each other in Pennsylvania.
We were chatting after church one week when the subject of my love life came up.
"Heard you might be dating someone?" Dave asked.
Wow, good news travels fast, I thought.

"Yeah, it's going pretty well so far. But we're not quite on the same page faith-wise. She's mostly an Easter/Christmas churchgoer," I said. "I want to tell her more about Jesus, but I'm not sure where to start."

"You could ask her to come to church with you, then take it from there," Dave suggested.

Sounds easy enough. Why hadn't I thought of that?

Tracy agreed to go church with me the following Sunday. When we walked through those doors, hand in hand, I was excited but nervous. It felt like bringing someone home to meet my parents. I spent the whole time trying to guess what everyone was thinking and praying that they all liked each other.

After the service, Tracy spent some time talking with Penny, who had invited her to get coffee some morning and read a Bible story together. On the way home, Tracy told me she enjoyed the experience and would think about meeting with Penny. In my mind, I gave Jesus a big high-five.

The following week, I took Tracy to a black-tie event. Everything was lovely and I felt on top of the world with Tracy on my arm. She looked stunning in an elegant black dress; her caramel-blond hair was twisted into an updo. We danced our heels off. It was a magical night already, but Tracy was about to make it even better.

During one of the slow songs, she whispered, "I met with Penny last week."

I looked at her in amazement. "And...how'd it go?

"Great." She smiled. "We're going to start meeting every week." My heart was doing leaps and twirls, but I tried to keep cool.

I wanted to stay out of the way so it would totally be Tracy's decision to get to know Jesus. If she was just doing it for me, I knew that would never work.

Months later, I found myself standing in the sanctuary wearing my best suit. I took a few deep breaths, trying to calm my butterflies. The church was filling up quickly. Ms. Ruth gave me a wink as she took her seat. It was heartwarming to look out at the crowd and see so many friends there to show their support. It was time to begin. I held the mic with shaking hands and thanked everyone for coming. Then I shared a little about Tracy and her newfound faith in Jesus. The room was glowing. I noticed the same sense of electricity that had been present at my own baptism.

The pastor's words were few, but I could feel the glorious weight of the meaning behind them. "In the name of the Father, Son, and Holy Spirit, I now baptize you..."

Watching Tracy come up out of the water while applause echoed throughout the church seemed to play out in slow motion. I was filled with inexpressible joy and an even deeper sense of belonging. God's family was growing and I was thrilled to be a part of it all.

Now that Tracy was part of my church family, I decided it was time to take her to the farm to meet Mom and Dad. It went better than I could have imagined. She really seemed to enjoy herself as I showed her around and was a great sport as I introduced her to my overwhelmingly large family. They adored her, just as everyone else did. Dad seemed especially thrilled and was more demonstrative than usual. I wasn't sure whether he was enamored by Tracy in particular or just happy that I'd brought a girl home.

Tracy and I continued dating for almost a year and everything was going better than I could have dreamed—until about springtime. Tracy surprised me with a romantic trip to Mexico, but things didn't go so well. I wasn't exactly sure why, but I had a pretty good guess.

Tracy booked a king suite for the trip, so we slept in the same bed together for the first time. She made it pretty clear that she wanted to have sex, but in my mind it was as if God put a huge piece of Plexiglas between us. I felt like I was supposed to keep my hands completely off her—we didn't even cuddle. I was tempted on many levels, but remained adamant about waiting until marriage.

We'd been home about a week now and there was a chilly distance between us that I couldn't seem to thaw. I didn't want to lose Tracy and could sense her impatience with me. Maybe it was time to make the big move. I decided to ask Tracy to marry me.

As if on cue, Tracy called. I knew I couldn't propose over the phone, but I was so excited—it was hard to keep my plans to myself.

"Hey, it's me…" she said, sounding serious. The fun-loving Tracy was apparently still in Mexico. "Can you meet me at the Corner Wine Bar tonight? We need to talk."

"Sure, I've been wanting to talk to you too."

I hung up the phone wondering if Tracy and I were thinking the same thing. She was a modern woman in her thirties—I wondered if she wanted to have the marriage talk too. Then again, she had been so distant lately.

What if something was wrong?

Things had been going great until this minor rough patch. I was probably just feeling paranoid because Jill used to drop bombs on me. Tracy was different. Maybe she was having trouble at work or needed to discuss a family issue. Maybe it was good news.

I briefly considered trying to beat her to the punch and propose tonight, but I wanted to do this right so I decided against it.

Later that evening, I sat anxiously at the table while I waited for Tracy to arrive. She looked beautiful as she came in the door and I relaxed for a minute. But my heart sank as I noticed uneasiness lurking behind her smile. Her eyes averted mine. I pulled her chair out for her and we both awkwardly settled into our seats. The impending conversation hovered ominously over our table.

"I'm just going to get right to this. I need to tell you something," she said.

"What's up?" I tried to sound lighthearted. "Let me guess, you need to confess you're a murderer—"

"David, I'm pregnant."

Every crisis alarm in my body went off. My heart beat out of my chest, my palms sweat, my head reeled. I couldn't believe this was happening—again. But wait, it wasn't even possible. We hadn't slept together. I could see her reading my mind as I tried to make sense of this.

"And…" she continued.

There's more? How can there be more?

"I'm getting married."

"What?" I said, completely confused. "We never even—"

"Exactly."

She let that sink in. It landed with a punch.

"Nope, I'm not the Virgin Mary and it's not miraculously your baby, David," she said with a pointed dose of sarcasm. "I'm sorry. I have to go."

As I watched her walk away, I went into a tailspin. I felt turned inside out. My heart and soul were sucked into a vortex right out the door with her.

I'm not sure how long I sat there. Numb and confused, I downed the last of my drink and then sat there some more. Sometime later, I tried taking another drink from the empty glass. The waiter asked if I'd like another drink. His voice brought me back from wherever I'd been. I shook my head to say no, and got up from the table. I wasn't sure what to do or where to go. But I needed to get away. Surprisingly, I turned to an unlikely source of refuge.

I headed back to my apartment and immediately called the farm. Mom was so sweet and consoling when I told her Tracy and I had broken up. I didn't go into the details.

"Honey, why don't you come home? It will be good for you to be with family."

In a daze, I threw a few things in a suitcase and headed out to the farm. It was Easter weekend, a time of death and resurrection. This sure felt like death. The death of a dream. The death of trust and hope—everything I'd been rebuilding in my life.

As I arrived at the farm, Mom came out to meet me and wrapped me up in a hug that only a mother knows how to give. We sat on the porch swing and I told her the rest of the story.

"How do you know it's not your baby?" Mom asked.

When I explained how I knew, she was speechless— probably stunned by this change in her son who was now so committed to his faith. She assured me everything would be all right. It was the answer you'd expect from a parent who doesn't know what to say. I didn't share her optimism in that moment, but it felt good just to be there with her.

When I headed back to Indy, my church family rallied around me as well. This was unknown territory so they weren't sure how to help. I'm sure some people wondered whether I would ever be able to consummate a relationship with a woman. But I knew I was ready and willing to do so. I'd simply been following the biblical model of waiting until after marriage. I did what I thought was right and couldn't understand why God had let it backfire this way.

Gossip ensued at the salon and in our social circles.

"Have you heard how she broke his heart? Of course, he wouldn't sleep with her."

"Told ya. He hasn't changed—it's nothing but a front."

Worries I'd once conquered struck back with a vengeance. It was like there was a bully in my head, always waiting to pounce.

See, you couldn't seal the deal. This proves you're gay.

Not true. I was honoring God. Sounds like a convenient excuse. Whatever.

Face it…you're always going to be alone.

I'd been learning to counteract the negative voices and fight back with God's truth, but in this moment, I was too weak. It felt like I was being pulled back into a dark abyss, questioning everything again. Maybe I wasn't healed. Maybe this was my lot in life. Maybe my dream of having a family and white picket fence would never happen.

I wished I could run away or hide under a rock, though I knew there was only one rock to turn to—Jesus. This was an all-out attack on my faith. I'd played a game of Truth or Dare. I'd taken the dare to trust a woman again and lost— *because of my faith.*

Why couldn't I have both? Couldn't I follow Jesus's truth *and* dare to love? Why did it always seem to end in pain?

HINDSIGHT REVELATIONS:
FAITH AND AUTHENTICITY

As I reflect on this chapter of my life, I can see how strong my faith was, even though it didn't seem like it at the time. I was committed to follow God's Word, no matter the cost. And while Tracy's betrayal may have taken me down, it didn't take me out. I didn't understand why God let this happen, but I didn't turn away from him.

It seemed like this was a great loss at the time, but now I know Tracy was not the right woman for me. God had been protecting me. Obviously, our relationship wasn't on the solid footing I thought it had been. Were her feelings for me real? Was her profession of faith real? Only God knows such things, so it's useless to speculate. But this does bring up an important point.

Our human nature tempts us to judge by appearances. Some people may act holy, but have motivations other than pleasing God. Other people may really want to please God, but still struggle with sin.

It's difficult to tell a sinner from a saint by appearances alone. Jesus was known to hang out with sinners and have harsh words for supposed saints—including the religious leaders who ultimately murdered him. Still today, some in the church may drift toward a tendency to focus on rituals and outward appearances, but these things mean little—if anything—unless a heart is truly turned toward Jesus. Only God sees the heart, so this is not for us to judge. We are called to love instead. Even those who hurt us.

I never saw Tracy again after the day she walked out of my life, so I can't say how things turned out for her. But I have forgiven her. I hope her faith in Jesus was real and that her betrayal was a temporary lapse in judgment (after all, I've had a few of those myself, even after turning to him).

Thankfully, the more I've surrendered my heart to Jesus and the longer I've walked according to his Spirit, the easier it's become to make better choices and live authentically. Not that I'm perfect now, by any means. But I enjoy much more peace as I let God continue his transformative work on me from the inside out, rather than trying to live up to external expectations in order to keep up appearances.

19

PICKING UP
THE PIECES

FORTIES

I HAD BEEN on the cusp of proposing marriage. Now, that dream was shattered. My heart was shattered. My confidence was shattered. Much like Humpty Dumpty, none of the king's men could put me together again.

My friends did the best they could, but only the King himself had the answer. With his help, the pieces slowly started coming back together. Jesus showed me that even though my past was forgiven, it would take more time to resolve my sexual struggles. My attraction to men wasn't magically wiped away by a serious relationship with a woman, but at least it no longer caused the confusion and angst it once had.

Same-sex attraction was no longer an identity issue for me. I started to recognize physical attraction merely as a desire of my flesh, not my spirit. This realization set me free. I could notice that a man was good-looking without wondering if it meant something about who I was. Ultimately, I had control over my choices—and I chose to do what I felt was honoring to God and his design for creation.

Instead of running back in the other direction in search of temporary comfort, I settled into the reality that I might be alone for a long time. Being okay with this helped me move on. God was enough. I was more attracted to him and his promises than any temptation or lie Satan tried to throw at me. I resolved to nurture the seed of faith that had been planted in me.

During this time, a few friends and I embarked on a journey to start a new church. We hadn't really intended to do so; it began simply with four of us meeting for a Bible study. We were an unlikely group. First, there was good ol' Louie, a Mr. Magoo-like character, whose antics always made everyone laugh. Louie convinced his brother Rob to join. Rob was recently divorced and came in very emotionally guarded (he made an announcement at our first meeting that he would *not* be sharing, but ended up being the most forthcoming of all of us). Then there was me, coming out of a gay lifestyle and recent breakup. Finally, we had one married guy—our youth pastor, Dave.

Our diverse group later became the model for community groups at a new daughter church that Pastor Dave would be leading. We developed a bond that God would use to carry me through a treacherous time in my life that would come many years later.

As I worked through the breakup, I was grateful for the welcome distraction that church and my career provided. My new salon became the talk of the town as my work was recognized internationally and published in national trend magazines. I stayed busy with plenty of work and social engagements and also purchased my first house. All of this helped direct my focus away from finding love. Of course, now that I'd stopped looking for it, love snuck in through the back door.

One day, a friend and I were shopping for a social event. A woman came around the corner and stopped me in my tracks. She was breathtaking, with mahogany eyes and matching waves of long, gorgeous hair. I was caught off guard when she smiled and waved in our direction, realizing I'd probably been staring at her. I awkwardly managed to wave back, only to learn she wasn't waving at me. My friend knew this woman from beauty school. And that's how I met Gail.

"You're a hairdresser?" I asked.

"Sure am," she nodded, smiling warmly. "Just graduated. Been looking around but haven't decided where I'd like to apply yet."

"Well, if you're interested, I have a position open. I'd like to see you come on board with us."

I didn't usually hire people on the spot, but I liked her instantly. I could tell by her demeanor and sense of style that she would fit in perfectly with our team. (Okay, and yes, I was smitten.)

"Thanks, that sounds great," she said. "Can I think about it and let you know tomorrow?"

The fact that she wasn't too eager to jump into something showed a rare level of confidence. I hated to let her walk away, but gave her my card as we said goodbye.

It's funny how a simple introduction can totally change the course of your life.

Gail joined my team a few weeks later. As I'd suspected, we worked well together and my staff loved her. Clients adored her too. Gail and I quickly developed a playful rapport. People often commented that we acted like husband and wife. I would always remind them (and myself) that with our fourteen-year age gap, I thought she was too young for me. Besides, she was an employee—so my rule was "hands off" (hadn't thought that through before hiring her). I liked her, but knew it was best that we remained friends.

Over the next few months, our friendship grew stronger. In spite of my reservations, we started spending more time together, even outside of work. I was able to be myself around her and talk freely about Jesus, the way Ms. Ruth had with me. Gail seemed interested and went to church with me sometimes. She wasn't a believer, just curious. Yet another reason to keep me from entertaining the idea of a more intimate relationship with her.

Gail seemed to have other ideas and often dropped hints that she'd like to take things to the next level. I was usually able to change the subject, but one night was caught off guard when she boldly brought up the topic of dating. In her defense, we were all dressed up at a lovely restaurant, just the two of us. I could see why that might be on her mind.

"So, David, why is it that a great guy like you isn't married? What are you looking for that you haven't found yet?"

She looked enchanting as she took a delicate sip of her Merlot, waiting patiently for my response. I tried to conceal my nerves. I wasn't ready for this conversation, but knew I'd been playing with fire as we continued to get closer. I supposed it was time to put some cards on the table.

"Well..." I stalled with a thoughtful sigh, "I've come close, but it didn't work out." I took a drink to regroup. "If I were to consider dating anyone again, she would need to have a relationship with Jesus—a real, authentic relationship. That's the most important thing to me."

"I see." She tilted her head slightly as she considered this. "What does that mean, exactly? How did you get to know Jesus?" Suddenly, this felt all too similar to conversations I'd had with Tracy. Did I really have to go through this again? I never talked about my past at work. It was a new salon with a new crew, so as far as I knew, no one—including

Gail—had any idea about my previous lifestyle. I wanted to be completely open with her, but was a little gun-shy. Talking about how I came to know Jesus, for me, meant telling her much more.

All I could do was say a quick prayer and let it fly, so that's what I did. When I finished spilling my guts, she was quiet. I was having a serious experience of déjà vu as I waited for her reaction. "So what you're looking for in a woman is a true commitment to Jesus. That's it?"

What? Had she blacked out while I'd been talking the past five minutes?

"Uh, Gail, did you hear everything I just said?"

"Yeah, I heard you. That past stuff doesn't bother me," she waved her hand to indicate its dismissal. "I mean, most people have a past, right? I'm more intrigued by this faith you have. It's rare to find a guy so committed to his faith that he would turn down sex. Now *that's* something."

I turned red as I shrugged and we both laughed. I wasn't sure what all of this meant, but was finding it harder and harder not to fall for this girl.

Later that week, I was folding laundry on a dreary Sunday afternoon. Gail had shown up at church that morning with her mom, which completely threw me for a loop. I couldn't get her off my mind—but still wasn't ready to go there. All I knew to do was take things day by day and keep checking in with Jesus.

A knock at the door interrupted my thoughts, as well as the chore I'd been doing on autopilot. I set aside the socks I'd been sorting and went to see who it was.

"Gail?"

Surprised to see her, I leaned in for a quick cheek-to-cheek hug and motioned with my head for her to come in.

"What's up? Thought you were hanging out with your brothers and mom today."

"I am, later…but I need to tell you something."

As she sat on my couch in Sunday sweats and a messy top knot, I couldn't help noticing (for the millionth time) how beautiful she was. I tried to push that out of my mind and listen as she continued.

"So I'm not sure if he told you, but I met with Pastor Dave last week. He explained everything Jesus has done for us in a way that affected me deeply. On the way home, I'd pulled over to the curb and started crying. I can't even begin to explain everything I was feeling."

Gail's eyes were glistening and her voice trembled as she spoke.

"Then, during church today, I had this incredible feeling that the message was for me alone. I suddenly felt like the only person in the room."

She paused, seemingly overcome by emotion.

"David, I asked Jesus to forgive me. I invited him into my heart."

Now I was the one overcome with emotion. I cheered and hugged her as if she'd just scored the winning goal. I stopped just short of putting her on my shoulders and carrying her around the house.

This explained why she looked even more radiant than usual, even in sweats. She laughed at my response and soon I was laughing too.

"So now what?" she asked.

"Let me make a few calls, okay? I'm here for you and we can read the Bible together if you like. It's also a good idea to get connected with another woman—as kind of a mentor. Sound good?"

She nodded and we hugged again. Logically, I knew I should have guarded my heart based on my experience with Tracy, but I couldn't help feeling overwhelmed with joy.

My feelings for Gail continued to grow deeper and stronger. We kept our relationship status as "just friends," but a new butterfly appeared in my stomach each time I saw her. Before I knew it, there was a whole kaleidoscope of them looping around, making me feel wonderfully queasy.

My heart had definitely moved beyond friendship. I kept having serious discussions with myself, trying keep the brakes on.

I need to put an end to this. She's too young.

Does age really matter? Live a little.

This is like Tracy all over again. I'm setting myself up to get hurt.

What are you supposed to do, never take a risk again?

My dilemma was about to be solved for me. One night as we were closing up shop, Gail said she had some news.

"What's up?" I asked.

"I've decided to move to Los Angeles."

"Wow." I flinched as my heart took the arrow, but tried to recover quickly so she wouldn't notice. "What makes you want to do that?"

"I've been thinking about it for a while. I've got friends there and they keep telling me I'll love it." Then she looked right at me. "I guess I just want to go explore and have an adventure while I'm still young...and unattached."

I returned to my task of sweeping up so my eyes wouldn't betray my feelings.

"Makes sense," I said, crumbling inside. "When are you leaving?"

"Two weeks. I guess this is my notice," she said sheepishly. "It's nothing personal, David. I've really enjoyed working together and getting to know you—"

"Hey…" I said softly, letting her off the hook with an acquiescent smile. "Go. Heck, I'd do it too if I was your age."

I sat on the couch that night, heavy with sadness. Although we hadn't been dating, I experienced similar feelings of loss. Gail's departure would definitely leave a hole in my life.

To shift my focus, I turned my head in a more celebratory direction and threw a bon voyage party. It turned out just how I wanted and everyone had a blast. Clients and friends came to wish Gail good luck on her new adventures. She looked so happy and I felt genuinely happy for her. But as I shut the door behind the last party guest, sadness began to creep back into my heart.

Only Gail and I were left.

"Well, guess that's that," I said, hoping to sound casual and lighthearted. "Sure won't be the same without you around here. Call me when you can and let me know what you end up doing, okay?"

"You'll be the first to know," she promised. "Oh, and I may have already found a church in Santa Monica. My friends told me about it. Sounds pretty great, so I'll probably check it out."

It warmed my heart to hear that she was making her budding faith a priority on this new adventure. It also left me with a sense of wistfulness for what might have been.

Getting back into the grind of work the following week was even harder than I'd expected. Nothing felt the same. Everyone noticed the change in atmosphere—I missed Gail and they knew it.

Gail and I talked on the phone all the time. The distance actually drew us closer in some ways as we realized just how much we meant to each other. At one point, Gail flat-out suggested that we should date. I wanted to say yes, but told her there's no way a long-distance relationship would work.

After a year filled with hefty phone bills and lots of "if only" conversations, Gail had reached her limit. She realized California wasn't everything she thought it would be—but mostly, she wanted to give "us" a chance. I knew for sure now. That's what I wanted too.

From the second she got off the plane, we were an item. Our age difference no longer mattered; we just wanted to be together. Everyone loved Gail and supported our relationship. I couldn't believe this was really happening.

I had a long talk with Jesus.

Could I actually do it? Is this the right woman? Coming out of all the things I've experienced, after all the things I've done—would I make a good husband?

I wasn't completely sure of the answers to those questions, but knew I didn't want to live without Gail.

It was a fairytale wedding, fit for a prince and princess. One of my Jewish clients was overheard saying it was the biggest "Jesus wedding" she'd ever been to. That's what Gail and I wanted and that's what we got. It really was like a dream. I'm pretty sure I floated through the entire event.

Best of all, I felt completely whole as a man in Gail's arms. The honeymoon was the consummation of everything I'd been longing for. Our sexual union was satisfying both physically and—for the first time in my life—spiritually. It was both intimate and powerful in a way I'd never known.

A river of tears had run wild through the valley of my heart for so many years. But now, the canyon etched by pain was filled with more joy than I could have thought possible.

Could this really be my life? It was as if God had opened the gates of heaven to lavish me with blessings—gorgeous wife, award-winning career, designer house, loyal friends, and a supportive church. What more could a man want? The vision I'd had long ago of having a family and white picket fence was a real possibility.

I focused all of my energy on being a devoted husband and felt deeply satisfied by my role of being a loving provider. It gave me great pleasure to pamper my bride with anything and everything money could buy. I was striving to do right by her and by God. We attended church faithfully. We joined a couples group.

Gail and I were happy together. If there were whispers of troubles to come, I dismissed them as paranoia. We may have had minor disagreements crop up here or there, but I remembered even my parents having arguments—and they'd enjoyed decades of being happily married. I was determined that nothing would interfere with my victory over the past, my complete joy in the present, and my hope for the future.

No matter what, we agreed to love each other until one of us went to heaven. Divorce would never be an option.

HINDSIGHT REVELATIONS: MARRIAGE

Movies and books often romanticize marriage. Yes, love is an important ingredient. But there are many definitions of love. God's design for marriage as described in the Bible goes beyond emotions and feelings, beyond romance or sexual intimacy. Marriage calls for the kind of sacrificial love that strives to do what's best for the other person. There was a revelation waiting for me in marriage as I experienced unity and intimacy like never before. This bonding of two souls was something I didn't fully understand then. It's a spiritual connection.

On a practical level, marriage serves purposes such as provision, procreation, and protection. Ideally, it offers a safe place for families to grow and prosper—and hopefully experience unconditional, reciprocal, sacrificial love. The Bible also suggests that marriage provides a context to fulfill sexual desires in a healthy manner. Imagining a society without marriage helps me grasp how important it really is.

On a spiritual level, God uses marriage and family life to mold and shape us. There are daily challenges and opportunities to practice selflessness in marriage. This kind of love doesn't come naturally to us. Giving up control doesn't come naturally, either. Marriage is like an exercise program designed to stretch us and help us grow stronger in the spirit.

Marriage is also symbolic—a picture of Christ and his bride (which is made up of his body of believers). This unity is the highest culmination of all things. Again, it speaks of sacrificial love. Christ died for his bride to save her. And as she sacrifices her own interests to follow him, she finds true love and true life.

20

FATHERHOOD

FORTIES

AS THE SHINE of our newly wedded bliss began to wane, marriage took more work and adjustment than I had anticipated. Little things that I either hadn't noticed or didn't bother me at first escalated from being minor annoyances to provoking full-blown arguments. Gail and I were both the babies of our families. She was used to getting her way. I'd been on my own for a long time and as the boss at work, I wasn't accustomed to asking permission. I quickly grew tired of negotiating over every single decision.

One day, after a particularly heated argument over whether I could have my own sock drawer, we looked at each other in dismay and wondered, "Did we make a mistake?"

We decided to seek counseling. As we expressed our grievances, such as which shelf juice glasses belong on, our counselor listened politely. After we'd both had our say, he sat quietly for a moment. I was waiting for him to take my side (since I was clearly right), but instead, he erupted into laughter.

Irritated, I asked, "You find this funny?"

"Well, guys," he said, reining in his amusement, "I hate to be the one to break it to you, but you're right on track. This is what marriage is about. It's give and take—or maybe a better way to look at it is give and give. Gail, let the man have his own sock drawer. David, let your wife put the juice glasses on the bottom shelf. Don't sweat the small stuff and you'll figure this marriage thing out."

Gail and I looked at each other sheepishly. We were both a little embarrassed, but a lot relieved. We left that day feeling reassured that we hadn't made a mistake after all.

So I got my drawer, she got her shelf, and everything seemed okay again. We still squabbled our fair share, but I took the counselor's words to heart and tried to let the little things go. Gail eventually took my drawer back and upped the ante by taking over the entire closet (since I couldn't be trusted to hang the clothes up properly). Even so, I tried to follow my dad's example of how he treated my mother—with complete adoration. The house was hers.

As we settled into our roles and rhythms at home, we continued to feed our adventurous spirits with plenty of travel. Gail wanted to have children someday, so we tried to see as much of the world as we could, knowing kids would take us on a completely different kind of journey.

Five years passed. Everything seemed to be thriving and growing—for the most part, our life together read like a page out of a romantic novel. And then we hit the first major trial of our marriage. It began with these words: "David, I think it's time we have kids."

This wasn't the first time Gail had mentioned the topic. I knew it had been coming. I also knew I couldn't put it off any longer without putting our marriage through serious strife. But I froze inside every time she mentioned kids. A big part of me wanted a family; that had always been the dream. Still, the past haunted me. I'd never fully dealt with the trauma of the abortion. I felt ready to be a dad, but perhaps on some level, wasn't sure I deserved to be one.

After checking in with Jesus on the matter, he showed me that this was another door to walk through toward redemption. He wanted to help me heal from the pain and lies I'd believed about myself following the abortion. It was time to come out of all of that and step into fatherhood.

Or was it?

Once I'd made peace with the idea of being a father, I assumed the hard part was behind me. After all, our romantic life was pretty robust. Making a baby would be easy, right? But after months of trying and waiting and hoping and failing, we came face-to-face with barrenness.

While I worked through feelings of frustration and bewilderment with God, Gail took the news even harder. It seemed that every one of her friends was popping up pregnant, and while she was happy for them, it compounded her sense of loss. I didn't feel adept at supporting her through this. Since we'd never shared intimate feelings in my family growing up, I struggled in this aspect of our marriage.

After much counsel and many prayers, we decided to try in-vitro fertilization. Miraculously, we got pregnant, giving all the thanks to God. The nine months both flew and crawled by as I did my best to transition into a new role, often feeling at a loss. Saying and doing the right things for the woman you love when she's a mother-to-be is something they don't teach men in school. Ready or not, the big day arrived. It was time to meet my child. After more than twelve hours of labor, the doctors realized something wasn't right. I called Mom (who had spent thirty years as a delivery room nurse) hoping for reassurance, but I could tell from her tone that prayers were in order.

As I fervently prayed to God to let my wife and child live, an adversarial voice broke in to tell me it was my fault. *You don't deserve this child because of what you've done.*

I fought back with truth the best I could, but fear was a relentless tide that kept creeping back in. I kept this to myself and tried to put on a brave face for Gail.

After a long night of worrying and waiting, Gail was rushed into surgery for an emergency C-section. The room went blurry and everything seemed to be swirling around me—in fast motion one minute and slow motion the next.

A nurse's voice echoed through my head. "We need to get the baby out, now!"

The next thing I knew, someone was putting a green hospital gown on me and leading me into surgery. I held Gail's hand and held my breath too. As my wife and I locked eyes, the sweetest sound my ears had ever heard turned my attention from Gail to the doctor. She lifted up my firstborn child.

"It's a boy!" she announced, as his precious newborn cries filled the room.

A son? My son?

There are no words for the flood of emotions and joy that coursed through my heart and soul.

I'd barely dialed the last number before Mom answered with an anxious, "Hello?"

I heard the barn line pick up too and knew Dad was listening. "How do you feel about having a beautiful grandson?" I asked, beaming through tears.

"Is everyone okay?" Mom asked. "We're all great—better than great."

They didn't say much more, which didn't really surprise me. But my oldest brother later told me that Dad had been leaning against the barnyard fence for hours, waiting to hear news. It was typical of my dad to be found outside where he felt most comfortable. What wasn't so typical was his reaction when he found out he had a grandson—he danced around the barnyard with hands held high. Not only had God given me a son, but he had blessed me with the great joy and honor of giving my father a legacy to carry on the Lowry name.

The nurse announced that Gail and the baby would be brought into the receiving room any moment. Friends and family gathered in anticipation. When they wheeled Gail in with the new little bundle snuggled safely in her arms, I could hardly catch my breath.

"David, do you want to hold him?" Gail asked.

A nod was all I could manage.

I cuddled him in close, terrified by how fragile he seemed. I marveled at how his entire tiny life fit in my hands. My emotions pulsed with fear and excitement.

Was this real? Could I be a father to this living, breathing, precious boy? Did I deserve him?

The past haunted me.

You know, you aborted a baby just as helpless as this one.

Tears streamed down my cheeks as I looked at my son in awe, feeling completely helpless myself.

Then I heard another voice.

David, this is how small you are in my hands.

I immediately knew this was God. Peace washed over me. I had the sense of being forgiven and cared for in ways I couldn't even conceive. In that moment, I felt that everything and everyone was going to be all right. Silently taking this in, I pledged to be the best father I could be, knowing I would need help from my Father above.

HINDSIGHT REVELATIONS:
A FATHER'S LOVE

When my son was born, all swords were laid down and unspoken bonds were formed. I finally felt like my dad was proud of me. To be fair, he'd probably been proud of me before, but this was the first time I really believed it.

By watching the way my father was with my son, seeing how deeply he cared for him, and understanding that this was the way he wished he had been with me—I was able to receive all of this for myself. There was forgiveness. Past hurts were redeemed. Our relationship was transformed.

When I first came out of the gay lifestyle, I'd written my dad a letter, asking for forgiveness and thanking him for bringing me up in church and doing the best he could by me. He never said a word to me about it, but Mom told me when he read the letter; tears had rolled down his face. These stories are precious to me. I had misunderstood my father for so long. As I released him from the blame, anger, and lies I'd believed, old wounds began to heal. We were able to move forward.

In my heart, it's as if much of our history was rewritten. I can see it for what I thought it was then, but there's a different storyline there too. I now see the amazing love my father had for me all along.

My view of my father and God was intertwined. I misunderstood both of them for so long, mistaking them as disappointed and detached. But their love was unwavering and patient; it waited for me. Receiving my dad's love was like a healing balm for my soul.

Unfortunately, it still took me awhile longer to fully receive my heavenly Father's love—I still had questions and misunderstandings to work through—but at least I was on the right path.

21

ECLIPSE

FORTIES

PARENTING proved to be both exciting and exhausting at the same time. It was intimidating to take our little bundle home, realizing we were on our own now. But we weren't really. God was there every step of the way. He designed babies and parents to innately work together to figure things out.

In time, we learned what each cry meant and tended to our son's needs. Through midnight feedings and endless diaper changes, Gail and I embraced parenting with everything we had in us. We rejoiced as our growing boy hit every milestone. In fact, Gail was so enthralled with motherhood that by the time our son was a toddler she was ready to try for another baby.

I was a little daunted by the prospect, but wanted my son to have a sibling. I trusted that God would see us through the in vitro process again and knew he was the giver of good gifts—sometimes even beyond what we ask for.

I stood in the examining room, watching the doctor check Gail's blood pressure and waiting nervously for him to confirm the heartbeat of my second child.

"Everything sounds good to me, guys," he said, with a curious smile on his face.

Before I could finish my sigh of relief, he adjusted the stethoscope on Gail's stomach and dropped the bombshell.

"Do want to hear the other heartbeat too?"

My knees buckled underneath me and I had to grab the chair beside me to steady myself. Twins? I'd known this was a possibility with in-vitro, but all the same was awash in a state of bewilderment, joy—and terror. Two babies? At once? Suddenly, an even more terrifying thought occurred to me.

"Doctor," I said, "please tell me there's not more than two babies in there."

"No, David. That's it."

I'm not sure what kind of look was on my face, but whatever it was caused Gail and the doctor to burst into laughter.

Our families were overjoyed by the news. As weeks passed, anticipation continued to mount as Gail's belly grew larger (and larger!) with our twins.

However, the excitement of pregnancy became partially eclipsed by worry when Gail's mother, Nancy, was diagnosed with cancer. We were told her chances of survival were slim. This hit all of us hard, especially Gail, who was very close to her mom. I adored Nancy too. She spent a lot of time with us and we enjoyed working in the kitchen together. As Gail watched her mom go through surgery and chemotherapy, it affected her deeply in ways I didn't fully recognize at the time.

On top of all of this, we were in the process of building our dream home to accommodate our growing family. The stress of it all put Gail on bed rest for the last two months of her pregnancy. I did my best to be a stable rock of support for Gail during this time. But the strain was wearing on me too. And oftentimes, Gail began to seem closed off and didn't want my help.

DAVID L. LOWRY

I prayed for strength and pinned my hopes on the notion that once the house was finished and the babies were delivered safely, things would settle down a bit. How quickly I'd forgotten what it was like to care for a newborn (much less two!).

The day finally came. It felt like we'd been waiting forever for these babies and at the same time, it felt like I'd just been in this very room when my son was delivered. Gail had been scheduled for another C-section, which wasn't ideal, but at least we knew what to expect this time. There were still surprises ahead since we hadn't discovered our babies' genders yet—but we were about to find out.

"It's a boy!" the doctor revealed, holding up the first twin.

This was wonderful news, but I knew how much Gail wanted a girl too. I also knew she would want to keep having babies until we had a girl.

Oh please, God, let the next one be a girl!

As soon as I saw the baby, I knew before the doctor said the words—God had blessed us with a girl.

Now our family felt complete with two boys and a girl. Even though the newborn days were a crazy-hectic blur, it was a time of bliss. Things could not have been much better in my mind. I had the perfect family and our perfect new house was almost ready too. Every prayer had been answered; every dream had come true.

During this time, I had a dream I hoped *wouldn't* come true—a nightmare of a massive tornado coming toward me. I didn't read too much into it at first, knowing that dreams can have various influences and be interpreted in many ways. However, this particular nightmare stuck with me. I wasn't fearful, but tucked it in the back of my mind, wondering what it might mean (if anything).

I was about to find out. A storm was indeed brewing on the horizon.

September 11, 2001, was to be a wonderful day for our now-larger family—moving day. I awoke thinking that I should feel excited, but even after two cups of strong black coffee, I couldn't seem to shake the heaviness I felt. Although there was no reason to believe this day would become a benchmark from which many losses might be measured, I must have sensed this somehow.

As I pulled into the freshly paved driveway of our new home, my cell rang. I saw Louie's name on the caller ID.

"What's up, Louie?"

"Hey. You have the TV on?" Louie's voice sounded grave; my heart started beating faster at the sound of it.

"No, I'm in the car. What's going on?"

"A plane just crashed into the World Trade Center."

As the horrific news unfolded that day, we mourned with our country. Our long-awaited home no longer seemed to matter. I had a feeling of impending personal loss that I couldn't fully understand. An unnamed darkness had begun to creep into the tiniest of cracks of our lives and sought to increase its territory.

During this season, Nancy moved in with us as she continued to battle cancer. It was wonderful to have her close, but difficult too. Over the next two years, she steadily declined until going to be with Jesus. Gail was grief-stricken and entered what appeared to be one of the darkest places of her life. I'm not sure she ever fully recovered. Grief widened the cracks, as a thick, inky sadness oozed over much of the remaining light in our home.

We went through the motions of life, mostly focusing on work and the kids, making sure they had everything they needed. But as I would soon learn, centering our world on mere provision was not the stable foundation it seemed to be. Gail and I largely neglected taking care of ourselves—especially our marriage.

Several years went by in a blur of day-to-day duties. The sun peeked through the clouds and everything seemed okay, for the most part. I enjoyed my career and adored my kids, so I had no real complaints. But once I'd been lulled into a false sense of security, another wave of storm clouds swiftly rolled in.

Though we didn't know it yet, the global financial crisis of 2008 loomed on the horizon. We started experiencing the effects well before it hit. In a blink, our investments, properties, and retirement were all in jeopardy. I'd been heavily invested in real estate and was devastated by the loss. Business revenue dropped 40 percent, almost overnight. We had a massive mortgage. I couldn't see how in the world I was going to provide for my family through this—not to mention my employees and their families. The pressure I felt was crushing.

Why God? Why are you doing this?

I've been going to church, tithing…donating to charity. I've gone on mission trips. I show up faithfully to Bible studies. I try my best to follow your Word. I changed my whole life for you.

What else am I supposed to do? Is it ever enough?

My resentment toward God was allowing a root of bitterness to take hold. The Bible story of Job, who lost everything, seemed all too relatable.

I began self-medicating with alcohol, looking for any escape. It didn't help. An overwhelming feeling of failure consumed me. I tried to hide everything from Gail, but she knew something was up. When I finally explained, she didn't understand the magnitude of everything we'd lost. So she didn't empathize with me; she just wanted to know what I was doing to get us out of this mess. This was the first time I started noticing just how far the cracks in our marriage had pushed us apart. Earthquake after earthquake had rumbled through our lives and the fault line was now visibly unstable.

I tried to console myself with positive affirmations.

I'm a good husband. A devoted father. I've done what I thought was right in God's sight.

But these attempts were no match for the voices that seemed more sinister than ever, perhaps emboldened by the dark atmosphere that had swept over our home. In my weakened state of mind, the accuser taunted me relentlessly.

This is what you get for your former life. These are your consequences. I spiraled back to the old days, plagued by the feeling of not measuring up to God's standards. I believed I was being punished.

In vacillating states of self-pity and self-loathing, I began to sink into a depression—though I wasn't even aware of it. Depression is a lonely, gray place that subtly envelops you, then refuses to let go as you're pulled deeper and deeper into the forest. Before you realize it, you're lost in a dark, self-consumed void.

The voices formed an unholy choir whose chants permeated this bleak world. They condemned me as a loser, and I believed them. I pulled back from everyone and hid my feelings. I knew that isolation was a dangerous place for someone like me—with my history and former heart wounds. But I neglected to consider how my emotional absence would affect my loved ones. I mistakenly thought I could handle this best on my own.

I just need to fix this and then everything will be good again. I don't need to bother anyone—Gail and the kids will be fine. Somehow, I'll make this work.

Besides...even if God is mad at me, I still have Jesus, right?

I reverted to my faulty "good cop, bad cop" theology. Jesus was my savior and friend. God was hanging me out to dry. My identity as his beloved child felt in question. As I lost sight of the truth, I fell for the same old lies all over again.

Is this all happening because I'd reached outside of my boundaries for a wife and a family?

Am I an imposter?

Even though my thought life was a mess, I never gave up. I waded through the muck each day, determined to get back on solid ground. Life with Gail and the kids moved forward and business gave me something external to focus on. I was still in recovery mode after the financial fallout, but stayed the course. Little by little, the heavy load seemed to lighten as each page of the calendar was turned.

At the end of the day, I still went home to a beautiful home, a gorgeous wife, and three darling kids. How could I complain? But sadly—though I didn't confess this to anyone—my attitude toward God remained bitter. He no longer seemed trustworthy, so my commitment to him waned. My commitment to Gail, however, remained intact. In spite of our emotional distance, I believed I could trust her to stay by my side.

Despite my misgivings about God, I continued going through the motions in church and at Bible studies, keeping up appearances. So it didn't seem unusual when Pastor Dave called.

"Any chance you can stop by after work?" he asked. "I need to talk to you."

"No problem. I can be there in a few hours."

"Okay, see you then, my friend," Dave said softly. As I hung up, I wondered why he wanted to see me. Probably something about the church. We often sounded off ideas to each other.

Later that day, as Dave opened the door to welcome me into his home, something seemed off—his demeanor, for starters. It took me a minute to notice that everything was silent. Usually Dave had music or the TV on. I started feeling unsettled.

"Hey, David, sit down on the couch, okay? Let's pray before we talk."

I nodded okay, but started getting really worried. I don't think I even heard a word he said while praying. All I could think was, *Something is really wrong here.*

"What's going on?" I asked tentatively. "You don't look okay."

"I'm not. I need to tell you something…." Dave looked up before continuing, apparently seeking heavenly support.

"David…your wife is having an affair."

"What?"

Surely, I'd heard him wrong.

"I don't understand," I managed, barely able to form syllables. "Are you sure?"

He nodded slowly, sadly, and put his hand on mine.

My head started spinning like the final cycle of the washing machine, spinning so fast I couldn't get it to stop.

The dark storm had reached the peak of its fury. The nightmare I'd had years ago flashed back into my mind. A tornado had come barreling straight into our home, our lives—and now I was swirling around inside it.

HINDSIGHT REVELATIONS:
LOSING SIGHT OF TRUTH

Before all this happened to me, I might have wondered how someone could truly encounter Jesus as I had and then later have their faith shaken—or even totally derailed.

At the root of our pain, addictions, and dysfunction are lies the enemy whispers into our minds. If we're not on guard, especially in our weakest moments, those lies can take hold and crowd out the truth. A life of following Jesus requires a constant returning to the "truth that will set you free."

Though I'd come a long way, I was still confused about God. Because of my upbringing, I was slow to receive the concept of God as a loving father. When things started going wrong in my life, it seemed natural for me to take it as punishment—consequences for my past. No matter how hard I tried to do the right thing, it never seemed good enough. I'd been conditioned to take on condemnation more readily than forgiveness.

I didn't understand that receiving God's grace isn't about being good enough or even doing the right thing. His grace and capacity for love, mercy, and forgiveness is so beyond anything we're used to experiencing. We often humanize God and assign him with our own tendencies to hold grudges and tie strings to forgiveness. It's difficult for us to comprehend everything that Jesus accomplished on the cross. It's supernatural.

Forgiveness is not earned; it's a gift for those who believe. But if we can't forgive—both others *and* ourselves—

this blocks our ability to receive the gift of forgiveness. That was where I'd gotten stuck.

The journey with Jesus is much more than a one-time encounter or salvation decision. It is a constant returning to the light. We forget truth so easily, especially when we are in despair. Lies often take root in isolation. This is why we need each other—authentic, safe relationships and community. It can be tempting to focus on external behavior rather than being transparent and vulnerable. This not only blocks our ability to offer and receive forgiveness, but also our ability to offer and receive love.

Thankfully, true love is *not* blind. It sees all—and loves anyway.

22

WHO AM I NOW?

FIFTIES

AS I LEFT Pastor Dave's house, I stumbled to my car in a stupor that rivaled my bar-going days. The drive home lasted an eternity, which was fine with me. I wasn't looking forward to confronting Gail. But I had to find out firsthand whether these accusations were true.

I walked in the door tentatively, suddenly feeling like a stranger in my own home. Gail was in the family room with the kids. My heart broke all over again, just seeing her there, looking so lovely. I could hardly bear taking in this picture of my family that I loved so dearly.

Please Jesus, let it be a rumor.

"Gail…" my voice came out in a choked whisper. I cleared my throat, struggling to stay even-keeled. "I need to talk to you, please."

"What's up?" She didn't even look at me, which was probably for the best.

"Come upstairs," I said emphatically, suddenly sounding stronger than I felt.

She turned to look at me now, probably taken aback by my tone of voice, but I quickly dodged her gaze. I walked up the stairs without looking back, then heard her get up to follow me. I sat on the edge of our bed, waiting. My emotions were all over the place from one second to the next. In this moment, I felt strangely calm yet overwhelmed by sadness, almost to the point of nausea. One look at her revealed the answer to the question I was about to ask. "Is it true?"

Gail's rich brown eyes that had so often warmed my soul now looked like cold, hard stones.

"Is *what* true?" she said, making sure to convey her irritation. "Are you having an affair?"

For a long while, Gail stood motionless, staring off into the distance as if she could see through the walls of our room. Then she blinked once in slow motion, giving an almost imperceptible nod. She exhaled audibly, but said nothing.

This silent confirmation unraveled my nerves. I looked at her in horror and confusion. How could she do such a thing?

"I don't understand. I mean, who in the—"

Suddenly, a terrible realization stopped me in my tracks. I knew. I knew who it was. Worst of all, it was someone close to our family. It was the only answer that made sense, even though it made no sense at all. My stomach churned as my nausea intensified.

I looked at Gail pointedly. She drew in a breath, holding her head and shoulders high in an indignant manner. I'd seen this move before. Gail didn't like to admit when she was wrong. But about *this*? Was she really going to try to make me feel like this was somehow my fault?

Calling on every last ounce of reserve strength I could muster, I did not take the bait. I did not raise my voice. I was not going to play the role she wanted me to. I simply shook my head in disbelief.

"What have you done to our marriage? To our family?" She said nothing but simply turned and left the room.

I spent the rest of that night in a fog. We were scheduled to have dinner with friends to talk about a shared spring break trip for our families. I did my best to hold it together through an excruciating conversation about future plans that should have been happy and exciting. But I couldn't see that far ahead. All I could see was the destruction left by the tornado that had ripped through my marriage.

After we finished the main course, I'd had all I could take and pulled Gail away. I told her to make an excuse for me and tell them I was sick. This wasn't a lie. I truly felt ill.

We drove home without saying a word to each other. I wasn't purposely trying to give her the silent treatment, but honestly didn't have a thing to say to her.

I pulled in the garage and went inside. Gail paid the sitter while I tucked the kids in. I didn't tell her good night. Just grabbed my pillow and went to the den. All I wanted to do was sleep, to escape my thoughts.

The mental shelter I'd built as a kid was dusty, but still there waiting for me. I crawled into my bunker, unable to cope. Every abuse and betrayal of my past rose from the grave. They joined hands and danced around my head, suffocating me.

Finally, in the early hours of the morning, exhaustion won the war over my mind.

I woke up around noon, wishing the previous day had been a bad dream. I still couldn't believe this was happening. Couldn't begin to process it, much less figure out what to do next.

Gail and I avoided each other as much as possible all day, keeping up appearances as necessary for the kids. News spread among our closest circle of friends—not in a gossipy sort of way, but out of concern for both of us. As people called to offer support, more information about what had been going on came to light. I minimized the affair as much as possible in my mind, but began to realize this could not merely be waved away. These kinds of lies and this kind of hurt could not be easily dismissed. I knew our relationship was in serious jeopardy.

We navigated through the weekend in a stilted attempt to go about life as usual, mostly for the kids (also because neither of us wanted to deal with reality). We even went to church as a family on Sunday. My emotions were at a tipping point. Too many people knew what was going on. But plenty of others didn't know, so we had to pretend everything was fine. I couldn't look right or left without feeling on display. Beyond that, church was the last place I wanted to be. I was not on friendly speaking terms with God.

After church, we dropped the kids off at a friend's house and then everything boiled over. The calm I'd been managing in my state of disbelief and numbness gave way to a storm of fury. Gail and I had the biggest fight of our eighteen years of marriage. It rivaled any TV drama—accusations and low blows flew from both sides then spiraled south. Each of us pointed out every possible flaw in the other, and probably invented a few for good measure.

It finally became obvious to me that any attempt to talk this out was futile. I needed to get away to sort things out. It felt like my marriage was being sucked into a vacuum and the only way to save it was to unplug the power cord, at least for a while.

My friends said I could stay at their empty rental condo. I threw some clothes in a suitcase, thinking a few days' worth should be enough. I left my home with barely a glance behind me; after all, I'd be back soon. Divorce was never an option, right?

I didn't unpack. Mostly just sat on the couch. Pastor Dave and other friends called continuously, but no one could help me wrap my mind around what had happened. I felt utterly alone.

My deepest heart wounds, once tenderly bound by Jesus, had been freshly ripped open by a chainsaw on high speed. I was completely raw—bleeding with questions and self-loathing.

Is Gail right? Is this my fault?

I wasn't good enough for her. Wasn't there for her in the way she needed me to be.

The accuser was overwhelmingly loud. In my despair, his lies made more sense to me than the truth.

Why don't you just admit it—you weren't man enough for her. You couldn't satisfy her and you know it.

Let's not forget about your past. You tried to run away from who you really are, but you can't change.

It's all catching up with you now and you deserve every bit of this.

The identity I'd built as breadwinner had crumbled, and now my title of husband was in jeopardy too. My confidence was being assaulted on every level. Sexual identity questions flooded back to the forefront of my mind.

What is left of my identity as a man? Who am I now?

All of the healing of the last few decades seemed undone—as if I'd been in remission, but now the disease was back with a vengeance.

I fell to my knees.

Jesus?

Why is this happening to me?

I couldn't feel his presence. There was no light. Only darkness. Only the weight of rejection. Only the sinister voices. My past became the ultimate weapon forged against me.

This is the punishment for your sins.
But what about the children? They don't deserve this.
Surely, this wasn't what Jesus wanted.
Jesus?
Where are you?
He seemed nowhere to be found.

A few days went by without progress as Gail and I steered clear of each other. Pastor Dave suggested that we seek private counseling, which we both agreed to. Unfortunately, it proved unproductive as we continued rehashing the same points over and over again, passing blame back and forth like a hot potato.

I knew I had to make this work. But how? For better or worse—that's what I'd committed to. That was my vow and I intended to keep it.

In the meantime, word of Gail's affair started spreading through the gossip mill, making its way to our circle of acquaintances, which included some of my old "friends."

I felt exposed and helpless in the worst possible way, a wounded deer taken down by a wolf pack. I was slowly being eaten alive. Meanwhile, the creeping things that slithered along the forest floor hissed with delight.

Wait and see. He'll be back for sure now. We all knew it was a front.

She was just a trophy wife. It was only a matter of time.

My fairytale world was under severe attack. Enemy arrows continued to fly and hit their target. All shields were down. With no truth to fight back with, I was captured and cast into the dungeon. It seemed as though I'd been left for dead.

God, do you ever even look down here anymore? Do you see me?

HINDSIGHT REVELATIONS:
WHEN GOD SEEMS SILENT

If a tree falls in a forest and no one is around to hear it, does it make a sound? If we answer yes, this begs us to acknowledge the difference between our immediate sensations and reality.

When I was in the throes of despair, I couldn't sense God's presence. Did that mean he wasn't there? Wasn't concerned? Wasn't speaking to me?

If you speak to a deaf person that can't hear you, are you still speaking? How about someone who's wearing headphones or is simply distracted—have you ever been ignored altogether? Are you rendered silent simply because you aren't heard?

Or if you wave to a friend, but they don't see you through the crowd, are you still there? Are you absent if you aren't seen?

Our spiritual senses are much like our physical senses in that they can be damaged, dampened, or distracted. Even though I desperately needed and called out to God, I couldn't hear or see him. I was spiritually deaf and blind—operating under a false belief system and overwhelmed by pain and circumstances. I couldn't understand why God would let all of this happen if he truly loved me. I thought he had walked away from me. I blamed him for letting it happen. And I blamed him for not being there for me after the fact.

There was only one thing that kept my faith from totally unraveling, and that was my history with Jesus. Even if I couldn't sense him at that time, I knew God was real. I had experienced Jesus's presence. I had felt his love for me. And I believed he was good. I was angry at him due to my own lack of perception. But I knew he still existed, the same way that I know trees in the forest exist and make noise if they fall.

That was all I had to cling to. Thankfully, that was enough.

23

RALLY OF THE FLOCK

FIFTIES

I LEANED OUT over the terrace with tears streaming down each cheek. The man in the moon seemed my only companion. As he wept empathetically with me, I longed for his sense of perspective and tranquility. I had no answers, no peace. My mind and body were raw to the point of numbness. A bomb had blown my world apart, my very soul it seemed. I had nothing left in me.

Jesus was still nowhere to be found. I concluded he was on vacation, or tending to someone else.

This kind of stuff goes on in the world all the time. Everyone's in pain, I reminded myself. *It's not as if I'm anyone special.*

As I considered this, a cloud blotted out the light of the moon, leaving me completely alone. A thick, heavy presence engulfed me as I felt myself being pulled down into that familiar dark, airless abyss.

A voice clearly said, *I'll give you anybody you want.*

I knew instantly what was being implied. It was an invitation, and a tempting one at that.

I could get even with Gail. I could bury this pain in a night of passion.

At another point in my life, I might have taken the bait. But even in my vulnerable state, the enemy's ploy backfired and instead acted as smelling salts, waking me up to truth. Something deep inside me rose up. Without hesitation, I rebuked these thoughts.

I told myself emphatically, *You will not go back.*

That night was another turning point beyond my understanding. Even while I'd felt all alone, a battle plan was being drawn on my behalf. A rescue mission was underway. The forces of darkness were no match for the army that was being assembled. My church family rallied to my rescue—a group of men and women gathered around me as true friends. I was a wounded bird, effectively shoved out of his home, lying vulnerable and exposed. But instead of being left alone for predators to devour, I found myself surrounded by an entire flock. Though I tried to crumple into myself and stay in my paralyzed condition, they wouldn't hear of it.

I call them my "bird feeders," because of the way they took care of me. They saw what my impaired senses couldn't see at the moment and spoke truth over the lies. They poured love into me, like a mother feeding her infant with vital nourishment. They counseled, prayed, and sat with me— not once, but week after week, month after month. They reminded me of my children's needs, which gave me something outside of my pain to focus on.

Alone, I was like Job in his weakest moments, questioning his very existence. But as I was called up by my friends, I experienced moments of strength and became more like Jacob who wrestled with God. I began a relentless assault on heaven, undeterred in my pursuit to save my marriage.

Weeks went by with no progress in my hope of reconciliation with Gail. It became clear to everyone that she had checked out a long time ago, but I did not give up. Our eighteen-year-old promise to each other became my anthem: "Divorce was *not* an option."

Surely, more counseling and time will make this work.

But I would soon learn that when a person has set their mind on taking a certain path, the situation falls beyond your realm of control. Free will is a lovely but precarious gift. Gail had made her choice, and it wasn't me.

Accepting the reality that my wife no longer loved me— and didn't even want to try to repair our marriage—bore a hole through my heart so huge that it was impossible to see any way to mend it. I'd modeled my marriage after my parents' six-decade-long love story and had fully given my heart to my spouse. When she didn't want it any more, the progress I'd made in my mental state was undone. The yo-yo had reached the end of the string and didn't have the momentum to go back up.

As my final reserves of hope began to wither away, my physical and mental health followed suit. Barely able to eat or sleep, I lost fifty pounds. I felt like an old man, so frail and weak that I welcomed my last breath. I found myself again contemplating suicide, as I didn't see how I could go on this way. God didn't seem to care what happened to me, so why should I?

But my rescue mission was far from over. A fresh wave of protection from my brothers and sisters beat the enemy back again. This was war, indeed. Winning was going to require multiple battles, various strategies, different types of combat, and an ample supply of ammunition. Even though I'd given up, my friends hadn't.

And whether I believed it or not, God hadn't given up on me either. In fact, he was commanding the battle station behind the scenes. There was a plan in place and he was faithful to see it through.

Yet even with God at the helm, my friends couldn't win this battle without my cooperation. Now it was my turn to exercise free will. I needed to re-engage. To rise up and fight. So I agreed to attend an intense counseling retreat which proved to be one of the most grueling experiences of my life.

For three days, I laid on the couch from sunup to sundown. The counselor scraped at my emotions, like he was trying to strip off layers of wallpaper, each pattern more hideous than the last. It was awful, but I sensed he knew what he was doing and quickly came to trust him. With each painfully slow advancement of the clock's hour hand, I was asked to dissect another piece of my life. I complied, determined to find the cause of my marriage's implosion. I had to figure out exactly what I'd done to destroy it.

The counselor's parting words were heavy. They hit hard, with a force that nearly knocked me over.

"David, love doesn't destroy. Your wife's actions reveal that she doesn't love you. But please know that God *does* love you. This wasn't part of his plan. But he can redeem it."

This was a shocking revelation.

My wife doesn't love me?

God really does? He can redeem this?

It was difficult to believe, but I did my best to consider it.

Driving back that night, I felt spent and subdued. But the burden of condemnation had been lifted which gave me fresh eyes to see God's love for me. I was able to turn back from the brink of self-destruction as I began to see how God had been working in my life, even when I didn't realize it. He'd been working through others.

My Jesus—who I'd imagined lying on a beach somewhere, checked-out with an umbrella-topped drink in his hand—was in reality heading the command post, with his sleeves rolled up and his hand in my mess. He was doing everything possible to bring good out of this chaos, directing orders to my family of believers, to my counselor. He knew the retreat was just the tactical move I needed.

In the following weeks, I gathered everything in my head like a puzzle. As I put the pieces in place, I was able to come out from under the lie that said I was unworthy of love. I did my best to accept the death of my marriage.

In many ways, the pain of divorce was more difficult to reconcile than a physical death. She was still out there. Still the mother of my children. Still someone I would have to interact with. I mourned our family life, our home, our joint friendships. Nothing would ever be the same. I saw the pain in my children's eyes and felt powerless to help them. Divorce was a multipronged, living sort of death—one that none of us would be able to escape during our time on earth.

But I knew now at least, that I could move forward. I believed, deep down, that God still loved me. This would not be the death of me.

HINDSIGHT REVELATIONS:
DIVIDE AND CONQUER

Divorce may seem somewhat commonplace in today's world. So much so that we minimize its potential impact. Some people mistakenly see it as the easy way out of a rocky marriage, but it's far from easy. Even though time has eased some of my pain—the divorce continues to be hard on all of us in different ways.

Divide and conquer is a classic tactic of a predator. Prey is much easier to take down when isolated. The enemy wants to break up families and friendships—to sow discord any chance he gets.

God works in the exact opposite way and urges us to stick together. There truly is safety in numbers. If it hadn't been for my friends, my bird feeders, I really don't know how I would have survived the divorce. They were willing to step into my uncomfortable situation. Even small things made a huge impact—quick "praying for you" texts, email encouragements, phone calls. Knowing that someone cared, that maybe I wasn't quite as alone as I felt, was my lifeline.

Some of my friends have since confided that they didn't know if I would come out of my depression. But they never gave up on me. It was one of the most amazing acts of love I've ever experienced. In the midst of feeling completely unloved and unworthy, people who had no real reason to love me, showed me how unselfish true love could be.

This is what I believe the church is meant to be at its core: people loving people. Loving them enough to walk with them—even through an extended period of darkness—and continue to shine God's light. To live like family. To flock to those in need and truly care for them.

Is there anyone in your life who needs a bird feeder? Maybe you're the one in need? Either way, I encourage you to reach out. Hope never truly dies, but sometimes it needs revival.

24

DO BAD THINGS COME IN THREES?

FIFTIES

I USUALLY loved the holidays, but not this year. I was dreading my first Christmas without Gail—without having our family together. I was also worried about facing my parents.

My eighty-year-old parents were both in fragile health and I knew the separation would be devastating to them. I'd kept it from them for seven months now, but there was no way to avoid the truth when I saw them for Christmas at the farm. I enlisted my brother's help to break the news as gently as possible. I knew it needed to be done in person. At the same time, I didn't want to spring it on them; they needed time to absorb the shock waves. Also, I couldn't bear to see their initial reactions firsthand. That would make it worse for all of us.

So my brother went to the farm a few days before my arrival to share with the rest of the family what had happened. My parents took the news very hard, as I'd expected. They wanted me to come home right away so they could see that I was okay. I was touched by this. The love of a parent is so strong, so lasting. After all these years, they wanted to be sure their child was safe. Knowing my father felt this way was especially redeeming.

This made me wonder if my heavenly Father felt the same way. I'd kept him at arm's length for so long, afraid of what he thought of me, afraid that he couldn't possibly love me—especially considering everything that had transpired in my life. But now I wondered...

Does he long to see his child too? To hold me and tell me everything will be all right?

I desperately wished this was true and believed it on some level, but couldn't fully receive it as a reality. If I had, maybe the pain wouldn't have been so bad. Try as I might, I had trouble consistently picturing God the Father any other way than distant and disappointed. Thankfully, Jesus was with me as I drove the long road back to the farm. I was terrified of facing my parents and seeing the pain I'd caused them.

As I guided my car up the familiar dusty lane to the farmhouse, I did my best to dodge both the potholes and memories that dotted my path. The task at hand would be difficult enough without being convoluted by the past. I put the car in park and took a deep breath. I knew there was no getting out of this, but my body didn't want to cooperate. I felt weighted in place.

Jesus, please...I can't do this alone. Help me be strong for them.

With this renewed focus, I was able to move my feet and make my way to the house. I opened the door quietly and walked toward the voices coming from the kitchen. Time stopped for a beat when I entered the room. I could see the shock on my family's faces as they took in my emaciated appearance. But in true Lowry style, everyone regained their composure quickly enough.

We surrounded the family table and talked matter-of-factly about what had happened and wondered together what life was going to look like now. Practicality was still the way of the farm. Dad was affirming but stoic. In his no-nonsense way, he seemed primarily concerned with finances and his grandchildren, saying things like, "Don't worry about their education. Your mom and I will take care of it. You just stay focused on getting better and doing what you need to do."

Mom did her best to comfort me in my loss, ensuring me that God was in control. As she spoke, I was no longer able to hold back the tears that had been threatening to push through since my arrival. I instinctively lowered my head to hide my face, just as I had when I was a boy. I couldn't help but feel the weight of the rejection that had started in this very place: the farm.

How, after all these years and everything that has happened, could I be sitting here full circle and still be such a mess? Would this ever end?

Whether real or imagined, I sensed awkwardness in the room due to my display of emotions and quickly excused myself. I felt the need to run to the safe house. The farm was like the epicenter of everything that had gone wrong in my life, a bubbling fountain of pain. I needed to see Alice for a reprieve.

Alice and I had stayed in touch via phone over the years, but it had been awhile since I'd visited. She welcomed me with a warm hug and I instantly relaxed at the smell of her familiar perfume. As I sat with my "second mom" in the kitchen where we'd baked so many cookies together, I'd hoped it could be like the old days when she seemed to magically whisk my worries away.

But this was a different time and place, which called for a different sort of conversation. Unabashedly emotional, I confessed my deepest fears and feelings of failure; I confided that I felt like I was losing everything. As she listened, slowly sipping her sweet tea, she seemed to see deep into my soul. I saw every emotion I was feeling mirrored back to me in beautifully composed empathy.

When I'd finished telling her everything, she smiled tenderly and placed her hand on top of mine, giving it a little pat. Alice said very little, which was unlike her. I sensed that she was holding back in order to be strong for me. As we said goodbye, she hugged me again, then looked me straight in the eyes.

"David," she said emphatically, "everything is going to be all right. You're going to be okay."

These simple words were exactly what my heart needed to hear.

Back home in Indy, I did my best to find some sort of rhythm in my strange, almost-divorced, world. I made it to work each day and not one head of hair was damaged, despite my tremoring hands and weepy disposition. I was also fortunate that my faithful core staff kept the business running smoothly.

My parents would call just about every day. Right before Easter weekend, after I'd hung up from a conversation with Mom, I felt the Holy Spirit remind me of a story I'd heard in church last week. Mom loved a good story. I thought about waiting to tell her when we talked next, but instead found myself redialing the farm.

"Hello?" I noticed that Mom's voice sounded tired.

"Hey, Mom. Forgot to tell you this story."

"Oh, David," she chuckled. "Okay, let's hear it."

"Imagine you're sitting in a courtroom, standing before the judge with your attorney. The prosecutor is accusing you of everything you've done wrong in your life. Your attorney asks if he can approach the bench. The judge allows it, so your attorney leans over and says, '*DAD*, didn't I already take care of all of this?' The judge ceremoniously brings down his gavel and announces 'Not guilty!'"

I waited a beat.

"Get it? Jesus is the attorney, and the judge is God the Father." As the full meaning sunk in, we laughed together for a bit. My mother always had the most wonderful laugh; it was like a pure shot of joy to my spirit.

"All right, Mom. I'll let you go now. Love you," I said. "Love you, son."

I hung up the phone, not knowing this would be the last time we would talk. Easter weekend, my mother quietly went home to be with Jesus. When my brother called with the news, I was looking out the window and saw a bright red cardinal—Mom's favorite bird—sitting on the bush.

How God?

How could you let this happen?

The two most important women in my life are gone. What else will you take from me?

My anger and disillusionment with God continued to fester. A few months later, my divorce was finalized. I knew life would never be the same, but amazingly, my suicidal intentions stayed at bay. I wasn't so much done with life as I was numb to it. A state of despair had become my new normal. I'd grown accustomed to it. I almost expected bad things to happen.

That didn't mean life got easier. On many days, I didn't even want to get out of bed. But I did my best to keep moving forward, for my children if nothing else. Praying and reading the scriptures continued to be my lifelines. I related so much to David in the Psalms as he cried out to God in pain and frustration. But one thing was different—King David was said to be "a man after God's own heart." I certainly didn't feel favored. If anything, I felt cursed.

The rest of the year passed in a blur. An old calendar came off the wall to be replaced by a new one. But I made no resolutions. There was no fresh hope. I felt stuck in a perpetual winter.

Just another year in this mostly gray life I've come to know. The lower my expectations, the less chance of disappointment.

Before I knew it, Easter weekend was coming around again. It seemed as though Mother had just passed. In fact, I hadn't fully processed her death. If my losses were customers, there was a long line. They would have to take a number because I wasn't planning to deal with them anytime soon.

The day before Easter began like any other Saturday. I sat curled up on the couch, sipping coffee while reading the Bible, as was my morning routine. The quiet was unexpectedly pierced by the familiar ringtone of my cell phone, beckoning from the kitchen. It was my brother.

"David, we thought Dad was going home to be with Jesus last night, but he's been agitated for some reason. He's still hanging on," he paused. "We think he's waiting for you."

Another pause. I couldn't seem to form thoughts, much less words.

"If we put the phone up to Dad's ear, would you talk to him?" my brother suggested.

Dad hadn't been in good health for some time now. The cancer he'd fought off had returned and taken a heavy toll, no doubt exacerbated by losing his beloved wife of sixty-three years. My mind wandered as I tried to process everything. I thought back to my recent visit to the farm. I went to say goodbye, knowing it would likely be the last time I saw him. As I'd knelt by his chair with my kids flanking me on either side, he grabbed my hand and squeezed it as hard as he could. It was a powerful moment. He was determined to be strong to the end, but this was one of those rare times when Dad was completely vulnerable and transparent with me. With tears in both of our eyes we said, "I love you."

I didn't think I'd have to say goodbye twice, but if Dad wanted to talk to me, how could I refuse? I suddenly remembered my brother was on the phone, still waiting for my response.

"Sure," I said, coming out of my fog. "Of course I'll talk to him."

"Okay, go ahead. He's on the line."

"Da…" my voice caught as I began to speak, but I was able to steady it. It was my turn to be strong for him. "Dad, it's me, David. It's okay for you to go home. You've been a wonderful father and I love you. Mom and Jesus are standing there waiting for you. It's *all* okay…"

I hung up the phone and let the tears flow. At least that was one good thing about living alone; I was free to express my emotions without feeling self-conscious.

Not knowing what else to do with myself, I wandered over to pour another cup of coffee and then stood there in a daze. I'm not sure how many minutes passed before the phone rang again. I didn't want to answer it. If I didn't answer, it couldn't be true.

But I knew it was true. I picked up the phone and my brother confirmed that Dad's breathing had calmed while I spoke to him. He passed peacefully, right after they hung up with me.

Sorrow welled up in me. Just when I thought I couldn't feel anymore, every buried emotion resurfaced.

I told Dad that it was okay—but it's not. None of this is okay.

Nothing will ever be okay again.

I was sure that God had decided to take everything and everyone I loved.

And not only that, he does it with flair, I thought angrily. *On Easter weekend again? Really, God?*

In less than a year, both parents—gone. My wife—gone. Three of the most important people in my life—gone.

Are we there yet, God? Are we at the bottom? How much sorrow can one man bear?

A voice in my spirit answered.

Indeed, David. How much? Every sorrow known to man, I have known. I bore it all—on Easter weekend, no less. You're not alone. You've never been alone.

It was true. I believed that. Jesus knew every sorrow and in fact took it all upon himself—every evil all at once—on the cross. My anger subsided. I felt humbled, remembering all that had been done on my behalf. The story about Jesus weeping over his friend's death came to mind. I pictured him there with me, weeping over the death of my dad. And then I pictured Jesus overseeing a joyous reunion: my father and mother embracing in a golden field, a place with no more sickness and no more tears. I smiled, thinking my dad would especially appreciate that part. No tears.

In the weeks and months that followed Dad's death, I couldn't completely shake my bitterness with God and was convinced he must be trying to take me to the end of my rope.

Very soon, I would see just how much God really did favor me. For one thing, I'd been given the privilege of ushering both of my parents to Jesus with meaningful final conversations. The Holy Spirit had known what both of them needed to hear in order to feel released from their earthly burdens and had used me to deliver those messages.

But right now, I couldn't receive this. I was blinded by grief—reduced again to functioning in mere survival mode. My bird feeders were doing their best to help, but I more often turned to painkillers and cocktails instead. I had to drown out the pain and could barely sleep any other way. I was lucky to get between two to four hours a night. The cumulative effect was devastating.

I'd hit a lot of lows in my life, but I must have finally reached the limit of what I could take—because God was about to intervene.

My father was dead, but I still desperately needed a father. I'd forgiven my dad on earth, but couldn't seem to reconcile with my Father in heaven.

It was time to meet God the Father.

HINDSIGHT REVELATIONS: DEATH

I've often wondered why Jesus had to die. Surely, God could have come up with an easier way to save us. Then again, experience has taught me that the best way is rarely the easy way. The things that I've invested blood, sweat, and tears into are the things that have produced the most beautiful and lasting results.

Jesus died willingly on the cross for us. It was a selfless act. I can't begin to understand the complete ramifications of everything that happened on the cross. But I have learned a few things:

1) Our sins were crucified with Jesus. That includes every mistake I've made—past, present, and future. Same goes for all of us. The Bible says that Jesus, who was sinless, was made to "be sin" on our behalf. I like to picture those nails demolishing all sin for all time.

2) Jesus defeated death. Eyewitness accounts confirm the resurrection of Christ. Those closest to Jesus while he walked the earth wrote about this. We're told that by believing in the power of his death and resurrection, we too can have eternal life.

3) By dying, we live. As we die to ourselves each day (deny our selfish tendencies), we're able to live an increasingly transformed life.

The death of my marriage and then both of my parents culminated to bring me to a new place of self-surrender. If I was going to live, then I wanted to live my best life. I had lived in survival mode for so long, which is a very self-focused way to live. But I'd grown weary of all that. When I finally shifted my focus to how I could help others…something amazing happened.

25

CAUGHT

FIFTIES

EVERY LIFE is filled with challenge and triumph, sorrow and joy, illness and health, loneliness and love, despair and hope. I made many mistakes along the way. I failed. I succeeded. My darkest days almost destroyed me.

But ultimately, I hung on. I was determined to discover the truth about God—and myself. I was convinced that I had been created uniquely to fulfill a purpose. Why I had to go to such lengths to find the truth, I'm not sure. My life so often felt like an overwhelming mess. Thankfully, Jesus showed up and together we mopped the floors of my heart, one chamber at a time. But it seemed that as soon as we uncovered the beauty in one room, I would come out feeling victorious, only to find another mess was waiting in the room next door.

And then there were the closets with padlocks on—the places I wasn't letting Jesus in.

As time marched on without me, I couldn't seem to move past the grief from my divorce and the loss of my parents. Friends started to wonder whether I'd ever snap out of it. I'm an emotional person; that much is written in my DNA. When I laugh, I fill up the room. When I cry, I cry hard. When I hurt, I hurt deeply.

In my spirit, I knew I could get through anything with God. Because the Bible said it was so, I believed that he loved me in spite of everything. But I thought of him as a benevolent-but-distant overseer. There was something keeping me from receiving his love on a deeper level, more personally. There were lingering questions. I believed God was good, but couldn't understand his ways. Why did he let so many bad things happen? To me, to others? Where was he when my grandfather hurt me? When I was abused, rejected, betrayed?

One day, I fell to my knees in a desperate state of exasperation.

Where ARE you, God? I NEED you.

Need to see you. Need to KNOW you.

The phone interrupted my prayers. It was Bernie, a family friend. We exchanged quick pleasantries before he got around to his reason for calling.

"Why don't you come over Friday night to hear my buddy Dr. Johnnie speak? He's kind of prophetic. I think you might like him."

Bernie was quite a character—unfiltered, impulsive— you were never quite sure what you were getting into with him. So I said I'd go, but not without hesitation. I'd never met a prophet. I knew people claimed to be prophetic on TV, but wasn't that all show? Weren't prophets mostly from the Old Testament?

I figured I'd go check it out and see for myself.

About thirty people of all shapes, genders, races, and backgrounds gathered near the lake to hear Johnnie speak. It was a powerful message. I found myself intrigued by Johnnie's presence and stirred by his words. Just as he finished speaking, storm clouds began rolling over the horizon, so we were ushered up the hill to Bernie's house.

As everyone filed in, I scanned the room for a spot where I could go unnoticed. I moved to a corner that was adjacent to the huge glass windows overlooking the lake. I watched as the wind began to bend nearby trees and make its way across the water, whipping the lake's surface into white peaks until it resembled a meringue topping on a mud pie. It was amazing how quickly the beautiful, serene water was stirred into a muddy, turbulent mess.

Story of my life, I thought.

I was in my own world, mesmerized by the drama unfolding outside, when suddenly, Johnnie's words broke into the forefront of my consciousness. He'd said something about praying over everyone individually. When Johnnie pointed directly at me from across the room, my pulse rate peaked, mirroring the agitated lake I'd been watching.

"And I would like to pray for you last, young man."

Seriously—what the heck? Do I stay or make a dash for the door?

You should definitely get out of here! Just sneak out while he's praying for everyone else.

"Young man, the Lord has shared with me that you have experienced much pain in your life. Please stay and let me pray for you."

That stopped me in my tracks. *Had he read my mind?*

Johnnie began walking around, praying individually with each person in the room. As he got closer and closer to me, I seriously thought I might be having a cardiac episode—my heart was *pounding*. But the moment he laid his hands on me, an overwhelming sense of peace calmed every nerve. It was like coming in from the cold and being wrapped in blankets of compassion, then drinking a warm mug filled with deep love and affection.

Johnnie's wife, Dee, handed me a Kleenex as Johnnie assured me that everything was going to be okay. "Here's my number, David," he said, writing his number on a piece of paper. "Please call me if you want or need to talk."

I later found out that on their way home that night, Dee had said, "Johnnie, I think you're supposed to help David."

And so he did. We started daily counseling. Over time, our relationship grew into a friendship that was characterized by healthy doses of the truth, spoken in love. Johnnie would often remind me, "You're running on emotions and religion again, David." Johnnie became (and remains) one of my most trusted allies.

In the meantime, my other bird feeders kept at it as well. My friends Becky and Abbie even brought me a little redbird figurine. They told me that, as a non-migratory bird, the cardinal is known for its resilience as it presses on through winter. The redbird, reminiscent of the blood of Christ, is symbolic of life, hope, and restoration. It was such a beautiful gesture. As I held the figurine, I wondered if I had that kind of strength to persevere—"the little cardinal that could."

The girls also seemed determined for me to meet their friend Margaret, who had been helped by a recovery ministry. I appreciated their hearts and intentions for my healing, but really didn't want to meet yet another Christian who would tell me what I needed to do or was doing wrong.

But they persisted, so I finally caved and had dinner with Margaret.

As we dined on steaks and made small talk, I kept waiting for her to ask me prying questions or offer advice on how to fix my problems. It was a bit uncomfortable having dinner with a stranger who already knew so much about me. Toward the end of dinner, she finally got to the point.

"You know, I really think you should meet my friend Randy over in Illinois…" Margaret suggested.

You've got to be kidding me. Another person I should "meet"?

Hadn't I "met" just about everyone by now?

"He runs this recovery program for men. I think the Lord is telling me you should see him."

This was getting ridiculous. Either everyone I knew was in cahoots, or the Lord was really up to something and trying to get my attention.

"Thanks. I'll think about it," I said, trying to sound more appreciative than I felt at that moment.

"Actually, his ministry is having a fund-raising banquet next week," she said. "You could go with me."

"Well, okay," I said, feeling resigned. I didn't seem to have much choice in the matter. "I'll call you after I look at my schedule."

Another recovery program? More talking about my past? Ugh. It was the last thing I wanted to do. But something—or someone—kept telling me to go.

Margaret needed to leave for the fund-raiser a day early, so I ended up driving to Illinois on my own. When I pulled up to the church, I almost turned around and went home. It didn't even look like a church, but was more of a metal, barnlike building.

Hope this isn't some sort of weird cult, I thought.

Rarely one to shy away from adventure, I decided to go on in. If nothing else, I needed to use the bathroom. I could always bolt if anything seemed *off.* My heart started beating faster as I pulled the front door open. I followed the sound of voices into a big open space where a few people were setting up for the event. A lovely, silver-haired woman looked up from her task of folding napkins.

"Oh, you must be David!" she exclaimed with a big smile. "Yes, I am," I said, wondering how I became so famous. "And you're looking for Randy."

"Right again." I smiled politely.

Her powers of prediction amused me. Maybe I'd stumbled into a fortune-telling convention by mistake. *Should I try to guess her name? Susan? No, maybe Sophia.*

"Let me call and tell him you're here," Sophia said. "He's over at his house, but it's not far. Can I get you anything while you wait?"

*Shouldn't you already know what I'd like…*was what I wanted to say. Instead, I went with, "No, thanks, I'm good."

Sophia directed me to a chair where I could wait. As I settled in, my nerves started to kick up.

Exactly why had I agreed to this?

I sighed deeply, trying to relax, wondering how I always managed to get myself into such strange situations. The roar of a motorcycle pulling up outside interrupted my thoughts.

"Sounds like Randy's here," Sophia announced. I looked out the window.

Whoa, that is not what I was expecting. So much for my powers of prediction.

I couldn't help but smile at the sight of a Harley Davidson, with a rider to match, and began wondering all the more what I was in store for.

A minute later, the "Mysterious Motorcycle Man of the Fortune Telling Church" (as I'd deemed him thusly) was vigorously pumping my hand up and down. I had to laugh at the absurdity of all of this.

"David? I'm Randy. Nice to meet you."

He had deep, gravelly voice and rough exterior, but very kind and gentle eyes. One of those grizzly teddy bear types.

"Mind following me to my house? Everyone's over there."

Oh, great. A group meeting? This just keeps getting better.

"Um, sure," I agreed. At this point, what did I have to lose? If nothing else, curiosity propelled me onward.

I stepped into a room of about twelve men. I marveled at the diversity of God's children and how he was the common denominator between so many different people with such unique dispositions. I started feeling more comfortable as I got to know everyone, and by the time we went back to the church, I felt as though I was among friends.

During the banquet, the men took turns sharing their stories of drug addiction and recovery. They each had stunning testimonies of the loving hand of God guiding them to freedom. I started to wonder if Randy could help me experience this too. If he could help these other men, why not me?

Not surprisingly, this wasn't a fortune-telling cult at all, but simply a group of really kind people who loved Jesus and wanted to help other people. I found out that "Sophia's" name was really Brenda, but I was right about one thing: she was lovely, inside and out. It turned out to be a wonderful evening. I was glad I'd taken the leap of faith to show up, stick around, and push past my discomfort.

As the event was winding down, I thanked everyone for their hospitality and started saying my goodbyes. Before leaving, I pulled Randy aside, wanting to talk to him about something I'd been working on—a book project.

"So several people have been encouraging me to tell my story. At first, I dismissed it as a crazy idea, but the more I thought and prayed about it, the more I felt led to follow through," I said. "I want to help people who were struggling with some of the same things I've faced."

I went on to tell Randy how I'd been working with a friend to get the basic outline of my story sketched out; how I wanted to help people find freedom—like he'd helped all those men I'd met tonight. How was I supposed to do that when I hadn't found wholeness yet myself? I thought maybe Randy could help me write the parts I wasn't so sure about.

"Anyway, I'm not sure where to go from here," I said. "If I sent over what I've got so far, would you take a look at it?"

"You betcha. Love to," he said.

I drove back to Indiana feeling very blessed that the Lord had put so many wonderfully stubborn people in my life who made sure I got where I was supposed to go. I definitely felt that the evening had been arranged by divine appointment. God certainly had my social calendar full these days.

Several days crawled by as I waited patiently for Randy to get back to me. Finally, Saturday morning, I got the call.

"I read through everything you sent, David," he said.

And...? I wondered nervously. Writing a book was way out of my comfort zone. I wholeheartedly believed it was something I was supposed to do, but felt stuck.

"You've had your share of pain, that's for sure. I think I can help you. When can we meet?"

I didn't realize that Randy wasn't talking about the book anymore. The help he had in mind was on a whole other level. I was about to have one of the most important "meetings" of my life.

The following week, I eagerly made the trip back to Illinois. As I parked next to Randy's Harley and headed up the sidewalk, a redbird in the tree to my right caught my attention. He was singing the sweetest song. A bird in another tree sang back. Others joined in. I enjoyed their beautiful music while waiting for Randy to answer the door.

"Come on in, David," Randy greeted me with a hug.

A few seconds later, his wife walked into the room, drying her hands with a kitchen towel. I'd met Lisa at the fund-raiser, but only briefly. She flipped the towel over her shoulder and reached out her hand.

"Hello, David," Lisa said. She had that same glowy quality about her that Ms. Ruth had. "Good to see you again."

I looked into her eyes and saw something different there—*felt* something different there—an overwhelming sense of love. It was palpable. A knowing resonated deep in my spirit.

I wasn't sure what was about to take place, but I knew in that moment that I was there for a reason beyond my initial understanding. I didn't realize it yet, but I had finally reached the end of myself—this wasn't about me. It was about helping others. But first, I had some unfinished business with God.

Randy motioned for me to have a seat on the couch while Lisa leaned over and touched his shoulder.

"I'll be in the kitchen when you're ready," she said quietly with a smile in my direction.

Randy acknowledged her with a nod, then turned his attention back to me.

"David, as I read your story, something became clear to me…" he paused, looking intently at me.

I caught myself holding my breath and let it slowly escape as Randy continued.

"I think the root of your problem is your grandfather."

Yet again, Randy had surprised me. I'm not sure exactly what I'd been expecting, but this wasn't it. *Grandfather?* The thought hit me like a cement block.

"What?!" I said in disbelief, a little taken back by the surge of anger I felt. "You're kidding, right? He's DEAD."

"*Exactly*," Randy said emphatically. "He's dead. But you're still here. So whose problem is this?"

I sat for a few minutes, pondering. Randy didn't say a word. Finally I said, "Well, I guess it's my problem."

"Okay, good. Now that we've established that much, would you be willing to go back to that scene in the barn with me? When your grandfather caused you to fall. As we pray, let's see if there might be a piece that's missing."

A few minutes ago, I'd felt ready for whatever God asked of me. Now, I wasn't so sure. Remembering Grandfather brought up so many emotions—not one of them good. It was easier to keep them buried, right along with him. It had been tough enough to revisit those scenes when I started writing the book, but I certainly didn't want to dissect the whole thing.

Randy sensed my hesitation.

"David, isn't this what you've been looking for? Wholeness? The truth?"

"Yes...*okay*, yes," I agreed, feeling more convinced as I heard myself say the words. "Yes, that's what I want. What do I have to do?"

"Let me ask Lisa to join us. We'll pray together and see if the Holy Spirit says anything."

Randy left the room. As I waited, I could faintly hear the birds still singing outside. A sense of peace warmed me like a ray of sunshine coming out from behind the clouds. A few minutes later, Randy returned with Lisa following close behind.

"Let's hold hands," Randy suggested. "While we pray, David, I want you visualize being back at the farm, unloading hay with your grandfather..."

Randy and Lisa began to pray and I started the journey back in time; it truly was as if I'd returned to the scene.

From somewhere far away, I heard Randy ask, "Do you see anything, David?"

"Yes, I see myself. I'm unloading the hay…I see the hay chute." It was as if I was hovering over the scene with a bird's-eye view. "Anything else?"

I watched the scene unfold. Grandfather came at me with his cane. I fell back, screaming.

"Yeah. I'm lying on the concrete, looking up at my grandfather. He's laughing."

My emotions were in full swing. I could feel everything as strongly as I had the day it happened. All of the pain of that moment, plus every bit of heartache I'd experienced in the decades since, threatened to choke out the memory. I didn't think I could bear it.

Randy's voice broke through.

"Still with me, David? What do you see now?"

I tried to refocus. Suddenly, everything took on a deeper, otherworldly dimension, as if someone had pinched the corners of the scene and stretched it diagonally.

"I see a white, hazy area underneath me—between me and the concrete."

"What is it?"

"Not sure. Maybe a cloud?"

"Ask God if he has anything to say about the hazy area," Randy prompted.

"Okay. God, what is that? What's underneath me?"

Silence. I couldn't hear the birds anymore. I couldn't even hear my own heart beating.

Time dangled in space.

Then…the most beautiful, quiet, loving voice spoke to my heart.

David, my son…that's my hand underneath you, holding you. I caught you, David.

If I hadn't, you would have died.

I sat in complete shock as the ripple effects of this revelation sunk in.

You were there, God? You caught me?

Wait…are you telling me that you've been at my side all along? All these years? Through everything?

You protected me?

I can't fully explain the extent of what happened in my heart in that moment. Once again, I was transported through my memories. I saw myself holding my own firstborn son, so helpless as I cradled his tiny life in my hands. I remembered hearing the voice of God, saying, *David, this is how small you are in my hands.*

He caught me. He held me. He loves me—as much I love my children, but with a more perfect love.

I understood what God had been showing me. His love for me had never wavered. I'd actually had the fatherly love I needed all along; I'd just been too blinded by pain, circumstance, and my own sense of failure to realize this.

I discovered that my pain *was not caused* by this loving God, whom I had so falsely blamed. I had lumped him together with my grandfather and father by assigning him fallible human characteristics. But now I knew he hadn't abandoned me. He wasn't distant and aloof. I wasn't unwanted—I was cherished.

I realized that our heavenly Father never created us to experience pain. I'd read the creation story in Genesis and knew that Adam and Eve had fallen for the lies of the enemy. This mistake had caused them to know pain. I always assumed God must have wanted it that way since He didn't stop them. He allowed it to happen.

But now I knew he hadn't wanted my fall to happen… so it made sense that he hadn't *wanted* Adam and Eve to fall either. He didn't stop it from happening because he created us to be free—free to choose. This means we're also free to choose poorly. So when Adam and Eve fell, he caught them too. And he sent Jesus, to catch us all. To save us all. He chose us. Will we choose him?

True love is reciprocal, freely chosen.

This revelation changed everything. It completely rewrote my life story. I had new confidence that I could trust God through every circumstance whether I understood it or not.

I was able to look back over every terrible thing that happened and know that God had been there with me. He didn't cause it. He was there—catching me, weeping with me, loving me—as a perfect Father who has a more complete perspective of what's ultimately best for his son.

I realized the same is true for all of us. There's absolutely nothing God can't redeem. He brings beauty from ashes.

Living with the realization that I was caught by the loving hand of the Father, was my most transformational "coming out" experience yet.

As I left Randy's house that day, I opened the door wide and left the darkness and pain behind as I stepped into the light.

A sunbeam kissed my face as I took a deep breath of the cleanest, freshest air I'd ever inhaled. I looked up just in time to glimpse a flock of birds, dipping and soaring together in unison. I marveled at how free they looked…

As free as I felt.

HINDSIGHT REVELATIONS: FORGIVENESS

I believe one of the main reasons it took me so long to understand God the Father's heart for me was that I hadn't been ready to forgive and let go of the pain of the past. As much as I thought I'd been trying to move forward, I couldn't really do this until I resolved the past. But forgiving Grandfather—and everyone else who hurt me—seemed like I was saying what they did was okay. And it wasn't.

When I changed my perspective from being internally focused to looking outward and wanting to help people, I started noticing that we're all in pain to one degree or another. My grandfather was in pain. My father too. Gabe. Ray. Jill. Carson. Tracy. Gail. All of us. People often react out of pain. And sometimes, those actions hurt others. Pain is not only toxic, it's contagious—like a sickness. But we have a choice: we can pass it on to the next person, wallow in it, or do everything possible to break the pain cycle and get healthy.

Forgiveness is such a huge part of healing. It's cleansing. It's sending the toxins away. Once I saw it this way, I was able to release my pain and give it to the Lord. I don't have to walk in my pain anymore. That doesn't mean I throw myself right back into a toxic environment. Some relationships are better kept at arm's length. I can forgive someone without inviting them back into my daily life. Praying for those who have hurt you can be transformative for your own heart—and hopefully theirs as well (but that's between them and God).

It's been helpful for me to learn that forgiveness is a process. I've found myself needing to re-forgive things I thought

I'd already forgiven. Pain can be like a disease—once you're healed, there may still be some lasting effects, or even a recurrence. The solution? Forgive again.

I strive to forgive people in the same gracious way that God has forgiven me. I'm not afraid to ask for forgiveness from others, either. Not just for my peace of mind, but for the person I wronged. Why not do everything I can to help them let go of the pain?

I've decided that there's no room for bitterness in my life. It's debilitating and it accomplishes nothing. Instead, with a renewed understanding of God's vast love for me, I steer my focus to the beauty all around me. And there's plenty of it, if only we have eyes to see

Epilogue: FREE

FREE

But not a single sparrow can fall to the
ground without your Father knowing it.
—Matthew 10:29

He found him in a desert land, and in the
howling waste of a wilderness; He encir-
cled him, He cared for him, He guarded
him as the pupil of His eye.
Like an eagle that stirs up its nest,
that hovers over its young, He spread His
wings and caught them, He carried them
on His pinions.
—Deuteronomy 32:10–11

AND THAT is my story, dear reader. Thanks for sticking with me to the end—which isn't really the end, of course. I've still got lots of living to do and plan on giving it my fullest all the way into eternity. I try to live each day remembering that I've been caught—in the very best, lifesaving way. I am free to soar.

You might be wondering what happened after that day with Randy.

Five years have passed from the day I started writing this book until the day I find myself writing this epilogue. It has been a labor of love and God's timing. My hope and prayer remain that telling my story will help others find the freedom and love I've found through the Father, Son, and Spirit.

The revelation of the Father's love for me continues to transform my life, through moments both extraordinary and mundane. I share custody of my three beautiful children and am still blessed by my work at the salon, as well as ministry and volunteer work.

With respect to other responsibilities, my children's schedules rule the roost. I do my best to love them well. We travel, watch movies, stuff our faces with junk food—I want our precious time together to be everything they want it to be, while staying within God's boundaries. My oldest is heading off to college soon and the twins aren't far behind. I am soaking them up.

If you're curious whether there's any romance in my life, I do go on dates, but I'm waiting for God to reveal whether another marriage is in my future. I'll remain celibate until such a day comes. Do I ever struggle sexually? Sometimes, sure. Celibacy isn't easy, at least not for me. But I don't struggle as I once did, not as someone insecure in his identity. I know who I am—finally. It's my goal to be content with what God provides.

I have continued to face trials, and lies sometimes try to creep back in. That worn-out reel of doubts and condemnation can still play in my head. But this I know: Jesus is with me, the Father loves me, and the Spirit always leads me back to truth. The truth silences the voices.

Counseling has helped too. I'm so grateful to those who have gone out of their way to help in my recovery. Without a doubt, my greatest comfort came (and still comes) from my time with Jesus, especially being in his Word. For that reason, to this day, I block off both morning and evening devotional time. I consider these times to be much more than a ritual—more like a lifesaving practice.

I believe when we give God an opening into our hearts (even the teeniest, tiniest sliver of opportunity), he'll show up. One way or another, he really will. Praying, reading the Bible, and getting to know God can seem confusing at times. All we can do is keep pressing in and pressing on. Keep knocking. Keep asking with an open heart and mind. He is faithful.

I've decided that only God's opinion matters. I try not to give too much power to the opinions of others—especially in regard to who or what they think I am or am not. I don't need a label. The Spirit confirms my true identity daily in my heart, telling me I am a beloved child of the living God, made in his image.

Seeing myself in this way has had a profound effect on the way I view my purpose in life. For years, I was the one continually seeking help—the lost bird. I realize now that, with a sort of victim mentality, I may have subconsciously wanted to remain that needy bird. The attention was comforting—sometimes painful, but ultimately restorative and leaving me wanting more.

But there comes a time to pay it forward. The time came for me to be a bird feeder.

God is able to use everything I've been through to help others. Having come out of many trials, I understand specific kinds of pain—rejection, abuse, same-sex attraction, sexual confusion, abortion, infertility, infidelity, divorce, death—in a way only someone who has experienced these things first-hand can know. And these specific areas give me insight into the more overarching questions we all struggle with, such as identity questions or finding truth and purpose in life.

Did you know that you have a great purpose in life? The enemy of your soul would love to keep you from realizing your true identity and uniquely beautiful purpose. There's seemingly no end of chaos and confusion in the world (and in our own minds) to distract or derail us. I encourage you: Don't give in. Don't give up.

There are people who want to help. If any area of my story resonates with you or stirs up questions, please consider yourself invited to reach out to me at comingout@usa.com.

Please remember, there *is* hope. You can COME OUT of whatever you're dealing with. And you can help others come out of whatever they might be dealing with.

You are NEVER alone. You are WANTED. You are FREE.

You are LOVED.

> These are the ones who have come out of the great tribulation; they have washed their robes and made them white in the blood of christ. For this reason, they are before the throne; they serve GOD day and night in His temple; and He will give them a home.
>
> They will no longer know hunger nor thirst; nor any scorching heat; for jesus will be their shepherd, he will guide them to springs of the water of life; and God will wipe every tear from their eyes.
>
> —Revelation 7:14–17 (paraphrased)s

CPSIA information can be obtained
at www.ICGtesting.com
Printed in the USA
JSHW020447060919
1292JS00011B/9

9 781640 884595